IN PRAISE OF *THE VANDERBILT CLUB*

Pete Mutch's book is a fascinating history of his family as caretakers of the Vanderbilt Club, one of many private recreation clubs dotting the rivers of Northern Michigan in the early 20th century. It tells the deeper story of the way a piece of property can capture a family and hold it for generations. And he writes touchingly about his hopes that his children and grandchildren will make new memories along the same paths his mother and grandparents once walked.
Honorable George J. Mertz
Circuit Judge
46th Circuit Court

This book reveals over 90 years of history of a family, the Vanderbilt Club, and why this is a very special place. I have been attracted to this place for two decades. Pete Mutch answers many questions, which only solidifies my love and passion for the club.
John Walters
Natural Resources Commissioner
Chairman of Michigan Trout Unlimited
Chairman of Pigeon River Advisory Council
President of Headwaters Chapter TU
Vice President Anglers of the Au Sable

Pete has gifted his readers a beautiful collection of vignettes that portray a loving family and their experiences with one of the most beautiful tracts of land in Michigan's lower peninsula. Be it interactions with "Pete the blind Elk", the mysteries of late-night visits during Prohibition, fishing, exploring, or simply understanding the simple pleasures of a caretaker's life, Pete has delivered a story worthy of your reading time.
John Porteous
Lovells Township Historical Society

The Vanderbilt Club

A Caretaker's Story

Pete Mutch

The Vanderbilt Club: A Caretaker's Story

© Copyright Pete Mutch, 2022

Illustrations by Nancy Mutch.

No parts of this book may be reproduced, stored in a retrieval system, or transmitted by any means without written permission from the publisher except in the case of brief quotations for the purpose of critical articles or reviews. For information or permission, contact:

Mission Point Press
2554 Chandler Road
Traverse City, Michigan 49696
www.MissionPointPress.com

Design by Sarah Meiers

Printed in the United States of America.

ISBN: 978-1-958363-47-8
Library of Congress Control Number: 2022920334

The Vanderbilt Club

A Caretaker's Story

Pete Mutch

MISSION POINT PRESS

Dedicated to all those
who listened to my story
in June 2019 on the banks
of the Pigeon River
in memory of Mom.

Mom (Patty Dudd)

Introduction

This project did not start out as a small book. My goal was to put some thoughts into some simple sentences and read them to the family on the banks of the Pigeon River where Nan and I wanted to surprise everyone with our recent purchase. I thought I would be done writing once that mission was accomplished. Little did I know that it was just the beginning.

My literary insecurities began years ago and were finally exposed my junior year at Alma College when the registrar called and told me that I wasn't going to graduate on time unless I completed the minimum English requirements—a simple task for most and usually completed during a typical freshman year. Up to that point, I had been comfortably immersed in the sciences and had always tried to avoid writing anything other than a bio paper. To satisfy this English requirement, I finally chose a literature class covering early American authors because I was told very little writing was required. Even though I enjoyed Emerson, Hawthorne, and Thoreau, I made a beeline for the bio building once the class was over.

After I read my initial short story to the family announcing the Club purchase, other missed events, further details, questions, people, histories, and locations begged to be included. I discovered a collection of relevant notations and writings that I made in the mid-1990s that needed to be dusted off and shared with others, not just kept to myself. I rediscovered many of the letters from Club members saved by Grandma and Grandpa Dudd during their twenty-seven years as caretakers of the Vanderbilt Club. I was even fine-tuning some of my story with Dad just two days before he passed away on October 7, 2020, at age ninety. I wish he could have read the final draft—especially the dedication.

Despite all my pent-up trepidations to author anything, what follows is an attempt by an uncomfortable writer to write a story. I spent the better part of three years researching and writing this story, continually adding to it and finding better ways to express what I had already put on paper—or more accurately, the screen. My goal and only intention for this writing exercise is to give the current and future Caretaker Club family, especially my three granddaughters, a special appreciation for how we returned to this very special place—the Vanderbilt Club on the Pigeon River. Anyone else who might stumble upon these words reads them at their own risk.

Nan and Me
Driftwood Beach, Jekyll Island, Georgia, 2019

> Sharing memories of those we've lost is how we keep from really losing them.
>
> —*Mitch Albom*

Preface

Over the years, our boys have asked that Nan and I record a little family history, perhaps some teachable moments or one-liners—those memories from the past that never seem to fade and live in our thoughts today. All too often we are preoccupied by our current tasks and tomorrow's mission, leaving the past to grow dim. Some of that past is what we would like to revisit today. It's grandparents, parents, siblings, wives, sons, daughters-in-law, grandchildren, extended family, friends, and experiences that help make us who we are today. So, it's on this occasion that Mom and I would like to share with you how the lives of our family's past have brought us to this particular moment in time.

> *"What follows in this book is an attempt to put on paper the many short stories my Mom has told to me throughout the years, about her childhood growing up at the Vanderbilt Club. I have to credit Ken Mudget with our writing inspiration. Just two summers ago, in August of 1995, my parents, wife, sons and I just happened to attend the Elkland Seniors luncheon with Bill and Ruth Horsell. One of the people I was introduced to was Ken Mudget. He asked who I was and why I was (in) attendance at a senior's luncheon at the age of 43. I told him I was here with my Mom who was Patty Dudd. Her name rang a bell with him and I proceeded to tell him some of her stories. Being the Pigeon River enthusiast that he was, he looked me in the eye, and in all sincerity said, "You better get all these stories on a tape recorder or video before she loses it." Little*

did he know that my quite youthful 65-year-old Mom was just outside his peripheral vision and heard the entire comment. She had all she could do to keep from busting out in laughter but decided to not embarrass Ken and remained anonymous. We've joked about his comments for about a year until we decided maybe Ken wasn't so funny after all. Mom said she wouldn't write an autobiography, but she would provide the facts and details if I wrote it. I'm not a (comfortable) writer and I really didn't like English composition (classes) all that much—but the bigger mistake, I felt, would be not trying. Mom still remembers a lot about her childhood, the people in the area and the Pigeon—she hasn't lost a thing."

Pete Mutch memo, written late 1990s

Dudd Road sign

> Tell me a fact, and I'll learn.
> Tell me a truth, and I'll believe.
> But tell me a story, and it will live
> in my heart forever.
>
> —*Indian Proverb*

Chapter 1

I remember Grandma and Grandpa Dudd, my mom's parents, living in Vanderbilt, Michigan, where Grandma Olga taught kindergarten and eventually retired. Grandpa Vern was a World War I veteran and had worked for the road commission and at Jack Demming's gas station. At one time he even managed the Vanderbilt Ski Club, the precursor to the Otsego Ski Club at Hidden Valley, co-owned by Mort Neff, the original host of the Michigan Outdoors television program. Before they retired and moved into town, permanently, my grandparents were full-time caretakers to the Vanderbilt Club.

> *"The Club dates back to the days before the turn of the century when a group of businessmen in the Vanderbilt area—doctors and dentists mostly—joined with a few Gaylord colleagues and bought an old lumber camp on the Pigeon River that was no longer in use. Sometime in the 1890s, maybe the 1880s, the logging camp was built. Once all the trees were gone, the loggers left and the local elite decided the spot would make a nice club. In the early or mid '20s, the Lansing Club (which is now the area where the Song of the Morning Ranch is located) was begun by some Lansing area automotive executives. Within a few years, some of their friends and co-workers had their eyes on making the neighboring Vanderbilt Club—just a short*

hike up the trout-laden Pigeon River—their very own. In October (Mom said April) of 1929, nine executives of the Motor Wheel Corp. in Lansing and their families bought the club and hired the Dudds on as caretakers."

Harold Times
Thursday, November 3, 1994

Michigan's early logging era was quite impressive. The practice of sustainable forests and replanting was still years away. Once land was cut over, the loggers moved on, leaving large tracts of open land dotted with stumps. Nevertheless, logging created tremendous wealth until the trees were gone … "The value of wood cut from 1849–1900 exceeded in value all of the gold produced during the same years. In fact, Michigan's 'green gold' brought in one billion dollars more than the California Gold Rush" (www.michigan–history.org). During the nineteenth century, Michigan forests yielded more money and created more millionaires than did all the gold mined during California's Gold Rush (Agilewriter.com). It seems that I have a distant connection to some of this activity. Mom's grandfather, Herman Dudd, was well known in northern Michigan logging circles. Herman died the year before Mom was born. Although she never described him as a "lumber baron," the *Otsego County Herald Times* summed it up best:

HERMAN DUDD DIED SUNDAY AFTERNOON

Heart Failure Was Cause; Buried at Johannesburg Tuesday Afternoon; Masons Have Charge

Another Otsego County Pioneer, whose home was near Johannesburg, passed away at the Gaylord hospital Sunday afternoon at two o'clock, of heart trouble.

About three weeks ago Mr. Dudd underwent a serious operation, and until last Thursday he was thought to be making rapid recovery. Friday he began having sinking spells and there was fear that he would not last the day out, but in the evening, he rallied, but his condition gradually became worse, until death came. His weakened condition following the operation, sapped his vitality to such an extent that he did not have the strength to stand the strain.

No man was better konwn through out the county and among northern lumbermen than was Mr. Dudd. He had spent many years with the Henry Stevens Company, having entered their employ as a boy at St. Helens' and was with them later at waters.

From there he went with the Salling-Hansen Company at Grayling, then to the Johannesburg Manufacturing Company, when the company was organized. Mr. Dudd moved to Johannesburg 37 years ago as superintendent of the yards and mills, which position he held until about ten years ago, when he retired to his farm on M-32, two miles east of Johannesburg.

The deceased leaves his widow, Mrs. Margaret Dudd, and three sons, Clarence of Three Rivers, Vernon of Vanderbilt, and Thurlow of Marine City, with their families.

Mr. Dudd and the Dudd home will long be remembered for the hospitality it afforded to all, and he will be greatly missed by his countless friends as well as his immediate family.

Mr. Dudd was born near Port Huron, July 6, 1865, and would have been 63 years of age next month. He was a lifelong member of the F. and A. M. and Forester.

Otsego County Herald Times

June 21, 1928

Grandma and Grandpa Dudd (Olga and Vern) were Vanderbilt Club caretakers from 1929–1956. This photo was taken in the early 1930s.

"Picture of me taken April of 1930" – Mom

"Peggy and me"
– Mom

(From left to right) "Uncle Lavist Anderson, Grandpa Dudd with me, unknown, Grandma Dudd, and Peggy" - Mom

Years & Places.

1916-17 Waters
1917-18 Meadsker School
1918- King School.
1918-19 Hallock
1920 Elmira.
1922 King School
1923 Wolverine
1924-25
1925 } Sturgeon Valley
1926
1927 } Vanderbilt
1928

1941-1961- Vanderbilt.

Total 33 yrs. 35

Salaries -

1924 - $900
1925 - 900
1926 - 900
1927 - 1000

1943 - 1200
1944 - 1300
1945 - 1350
1946 - 1500
1947 - 1800
1948 - 2000
1949 - 2160
1950 - 2250
1951 - 2490
1952 - 2490
1953 - 2490
1954 - 2800
1955 - 2900
1956 - 3125
1957 - 3125
1958 - 3275
1959 - 3500
1960 - 3700
1961 - 4000
1962 - 4100

Grandma's teaching records and corresponding salaries

Grandma and Grandpa were assistant caretakers of the Lansing Club when the neighboring Vanderbilt Club property went up for sale and caught the eye of visiting guests from Motor Wheel Corporation of Lansing. When the purchase was completed, the new owners asked them to make the short move upstream as full-time caretakers to the 312-acre Vanderbilt Club in April 1929. Mom (Grandma Pat/Great Grandma G) was born in Gaylord on November 28, 1929, and brought home to the Club several days later. Grandma had taught school for several years but stopped teaching when Mom was born and her full-time Club caretaking responsibilities began. Mom's sister, Peggy, made up the rest of the family. Most of Mom's memories and stories of the Club did not include Peggy, who was eight years older. She left the Club and Vanderbilt soon after graduation from high school.

Mom told us how the new owners came to the Club that fall to rechink the logs. The new owners felt that without these repairs, it would be too cold for a newborn. Mom always spoke fondly of the men and their families and had good things to say about the corporate attitude of these executives of Motor Wheel Corporation:

> "William Prudden is known by some as the forefather of the modern wheel industry. After graduating from Michigan Agricultural College and leaving Lansing, he returned in 1898 at the age of 39, with machinery and stock to begin a new factory, Michigan Wheel Company, to make rubber-tired wheels and his first passion, horse racing sulkies. After leaving Lansing again, Prudden returned to Lansing in 1903 and founded W.K. Prudden and Company. Prudden innovated the so-called artillery type wheel. Made with hickory spokes, it was credited with revolutionizing the entire wheel-building industry. Prudden Company was awarded a $3 million military wheel contract and began manufacturing in January of 1918. In 1920, Motor Wheel Corp. was formed from a consolidation of the Prudden Wheel Co., Auto Wheel Co., and Weis and Lesh Manufacturing Co., all of Lansing. Motor Wheel became the world's top manufacturer of both wood and steel wheels in 1924. By 1934, Motor Wheel controlled one third of the nation's wheel business. Its products were diversified, ranging from wood and steel wheels during the 1920s, to shell casings during World War II to water heaters and lawn mowers for

growing households in the 1950s. Motor Wheel was purchased by Goodyear Rubber and Tire in 1964 and later Hayes in 1996. The plant at 707 Prudden St., formerly 725 E. Saginaw, (Lansing, Michigan) was closed in 1975."

Lansing State Journal, *April 8, 2016*

"Probably the way the Club looked before the folks went there in April 1929. Mom and Dad had been 'assistant caretakers' at the Lansing Club, owned by executives of Motor Wheel Corporation of Lansing. Guests of the Lansing Club, also executives of Motor Wheel, learned the Vanderbilt Club was for sale and they decided to purchase it. Mom and Dad were hired as the new caretakers. I don't know how many men made the initial purchase, probably Messrs. Carlton, Holden, and Porter, but there were nine members through the many years the folks were there. In addition to the three names above, there were Messrs. Day, Walton, Fisher, Coryell, George Hagglemire, and his son Ralph." – Mom

By 1924, the company employed as many people as the state of Michigan did in 2000. By 1934, Motor Wheel controlled one-third of the nation's wheel business, more by far than any other single manufacturer (www.motorwheel-intel.com). In the 1940s, Motor Wheel CentriFuse brake drums were used on World War II aircraft and trucks due to their performance and strength. After the Goodyear purchase in 1964, Motor Wheel eventually moved from Lansing to Chattanooga, Tennessee, in 1986. Most recently, Motor Wheel was acquired by Hendrickson Commercial Vehicle Systems in 2020.

The caretakers' job provided the family with a roof over their heads and a modest monthly income of seventy-five dollars—today's equivalent of $1,169.79 per month. It's interesting to note that their Club salary in 1929 ($900) almost matched the salary Grandma made teaching the year before ($1,000). However, during the depths of the Depression, their salary was withheld. During those lean times, Grandma's brother, Uncle Lauist Anderson, a pharmacist who worked for Glassers Pharmacy in Gaylord, would lend a little financial support when they needed some extra help.

Mom remembers a "black vehicle" arriving with bottles of "something" that Grandpa would quickly hide in the safe near the fireplace. The members also liked their beer. She remembers stirring the homemade brew and skimming off the foam. The pigs, Maggie and Jigs, would occasionally find the foam and eagerly lick it up. In a short time, the pigs could be pretty entertaining!

Mom would have been only four years old when Prohibition ended on December 5, 1933, with the passage of the 21st amendment to the U.S. Constitution to legalize the production, transportation, and sale of alcohol which had been previously outlawed on January 17, 1920, with the passage of the 18th amendment. I never did ask if all her moonshine memories took place during or shortly after Prohibition. Judging by the way she always described these clandestine activities, I suspect it was a little of both.

There was a gun in the corner by the back door to ward off those who were ever tempted to steal from the Club. Mom recalled one incident during World War II when someone was attempting to steal highly rationed fuel oil. Grandma opened the door and pointed the gun. The troublemakers quickly left the property.

During my grandparents' caretaking years, members used the Club to entertain guests, business clients, and even politicians. James Doolittle, famed World War II air commander and Air Force four star general planned

Club members at the dining room table

This bell was used inside the Club house to get Grandma's attention.

on visiting the Club, but cancelled at the last minute. More importantly the Club was a place to get away with family and friends for some downtime and good food. Grandma, Grandpa, and Mom always spoke fondly of all the Club members and had a very personal relationship with many of them. In turn, the members, as reflected in their letters, loved how they were treated once they arrived and how they hated to leave. They especially marveled at Grandma's cooking. I still have the bell that was used around the Club and at the dining room table when members needed Grandma's assistance or a second helping.

Grandma saved many of the letters Club members wrote to them during their twenty-seven years as caretakers. The letters not only reveal the different business and management styles of each Club member, but the letters also expose their personal sides. Many of the letters, including the initial work contract, were from C.C. Carlton, acting Club Chairman. Letters from other members and guests were also saved, spanning a period of time from April 22, 1929, to October 8, 1956, beginning with the Great Depression, through World War II, into the economic boom times of the 1950s, and ending with the passing of a key Club member.

These were challenging times for our nation, businesses, and people. Our nation's Great Depression got its start just months after the Club was purchased. On October 24, 1929, Black Thursday, the stock market crashed. It continued to slide for nearly three more years until it bottomed on July 8, 1932. It lost 90 percent of its value from its peak on September 3, 1929. It didn't reach that high again until twenty-five years later. The Great Depression created a national unemployment rate of 25 percent by 1933.

The Great Depression finally ended as America became more involved in World War II, initially supporting Britain and France in their struggle against Germany and other Axis Powers that began in September 1939. America finally entered the war in December 1941.

Motor Wheel Corporation was able to survive. Many aircraft and tanks used Motor Wheel parts due to their superior performance and strength. A national economic recovery was finally in place as factories began to reopen and America went back to work to support the war effort.

However, during the war, citizens were asked to make many sacrifices and were given a series of ration cards and stamps. Rations were placed on critical household items and the coupons were needed to purchase meager amounts of meat, dairy, coffee, dried fruits, jams, lard, shortening, and oils. Some items were added or deleted depending on availability. By the end of 1942, ration coupons were used for other items such as typewriters, gasoline, bicycles, shoes, rubber, footwear, silk, nylon, fuel oil, and stones.

Ration booklet samples

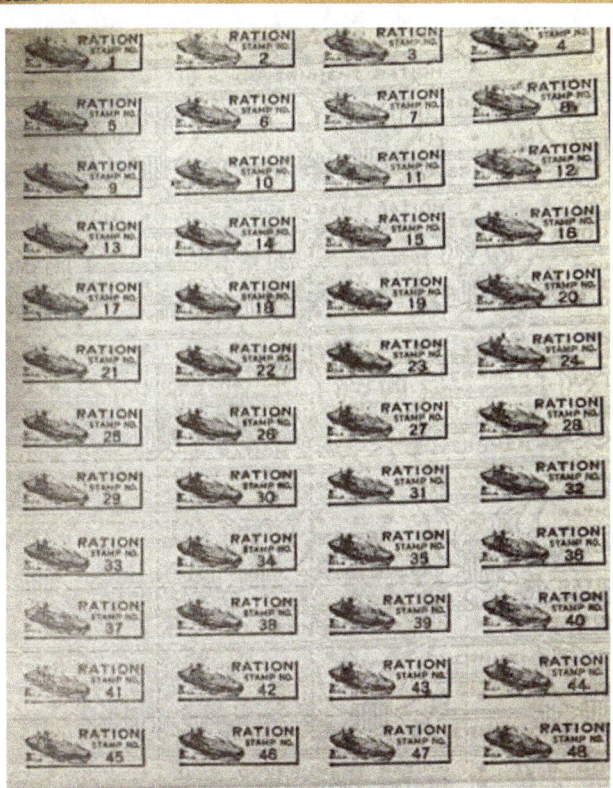

Not only was gasoline rationed, but a national Victory speed limit of thirty-five miles per hour was imposed to conserve rubber. Car manufacturing was stopped on January 1, 1942. The auto industry began producing jeeps, tanks, and bombers, until car manufacturing resumed on July 1, 1945. The war finally ended on September 2, 1945. When the 1950s began, the economy was booming.

It was against these conditions and backdrop that most of the following letters were written.

> **Pat**
>
> 2-24-84
>
> *[handwritten note, partially legible]* After this many years I am going through papers of the folks that I have had stored away upstairs in a cupboard — just as I brought them from the home in Vanderbilt. Now it is not quite so painful to sort through the memories but it is a lonely task. There is no one to share. These memories are only important to me. Hence if the letters contained in this packet are of interest to you, I have made some notations on each, keep them otherwise throw them away. The letters in this particular file pertain mainly to life at the Vanderbilt Club from the time Grandpa and Grandma went there in Sept of 1929 until the Club was sold to Mr. Ginnard in October of 1956.

This notation from Mom, dated February 24, 1984, was found in a box of saved letters from Club members and some guests. We always teased Mom about her handwriting. It was always small and got smaller as she got older.

MOTOR WHEEL CORPORATION

MOTOR VEHICLE WHEELS COMPLETE
PRESSED STEEL PRODUCTS ~ VEHICLE WOODSTOCK

LANSING, MICHIGAN

April 22, 1929.

Mr. and Mrs. Vern Dud,
C/o Vanderbilt Club,
Vanderbilt, Michigan.

Dear Mr. and Mrs. Dud:

It will be more satisfactory to you as well as to all of the Club members if we have our arrangement for the coming year in writing.

For your information I enclose a copy of the agreement that we had with Mr. and Mrs. Rich for last year, in order that you may compare the following agreement that I have written you with the one which they had last year, and you will note that your agreement is considerably more advantageous to you than theirs was to them.

EMPLOYMENT: Your year will start April 15, 1929 and end on April 14, 1930. You actually started April 20th, but we are dating back to April 15th because of the fact that you were kind enough to come out and take care of things for us over the last week-end and because you have so much extra work to do getting cleaned up in such a short time.

DUTIES: You are to act as keepers of the Vanderbilt Club, in full charge of all Club property. You are to keep everything in first class order and furnish whatever help is necessary to take care of members and their guests while they are there. You will furnish all food for members and their guests, and each member will pay you at the rate of two dollars ($2.00) per day for board for himself and each guest while there. Each member will settle with you for his own meals and the meals of his guests at the time he leaves the Club.

You are to furnish an automobile to take members and guests to and from trains as they wish, and do whatever guide work is necessary and possible for you to handle. If additional

MOTOR WHEEL CORPORATION

SHEET NO. 2.

Mr. and Mrs. Vern Dud
4-22-29

guide work is required you will arrange, upon the request of any member, with Jess or Frank Rich for such extra guide help. We have been paying the Rich brothers on the basis of eight dollars ($8.00) per day for a guide with a car and five dollars ($5.00) per day for a guide without a car.

We have already paid Jess Rich for our ice supply for the 1929 season. You are to deliver the ice to the Club and be sure the ice box is filled whenever members and guests are there.

You are to take care of all general Club laundry, such as sheets, pillow cases, blankets, towels and table linen, and you are to do any personal laundry for members and guests which they require, for which members will pay you at regular laundry rates which can be agreed upon between you and the members. There will be very little of this personal laundry.

COMPENSATION: For acting as keepers of the Club we are to pay you five hundred dollars ($500.00) per year, at the rate of $41.66-2/3 per month, and for your car and guide work and other services an additional four hundred dollars ($400.00) per year at the rate of $33.33-1/3 per month, making a total of $75.00 per month for twelve (12) months.

The Treasurer of the Club is C. M. Day, Jaxon Steel Products Company, Jackson, Michigan. I have talked with Mr. Day over the telephone this morning, and he will send you this week your first check for $75.00, covering the month from April 15th to May 15th, and Mr. Day will send you a check for $75.00 on the 15th day of each month thereafter.

MEALS: As mentioned above, you will charge members and members' guests two dollars ($2.00) per day. In the case of single meals only the following schedule will be used: Breakfast, 75¢; Lunch, 50¢; Dinner, $1.00.

FUEL: The Club will furnish wood for the fireplace and oil for the water heater, and oil for the room heater in the dining room. You will furnish fuel for your own cook stove. The Club will also furnish gasoline for the motor on the lighting system.

MOTOR WHEEL CORPORATION

SHEET NO. 3.

Mr. and Mrs. Vern Dud
4-22-29

BILLS: All miscellaneous bills which you have to pay, such as telephone bills, gasoline bills, oil bills and miscellaneous supplies which it is agreed that you should purchase, should be sent to C. C. Carlton, Motor Wheel Corporation, Lansing, Michigan, who is acting as chairman of the House Committee this year. I will O. K. such bills promptly and send them to Mr. Day, and you will receive all checks from Mr. Day as Treasurer of the Club.

ADDITIONAL HELP FOR CLEANING: As I agreed with you a few days ago, the Club needs a lot of cleaning and you will hire this week and next such additional help as is necessary to assist you in getting the place in as fine condition as possible before the members come up for the opening on May 3d. You will no doubt be able to give me bills for this extra labor and such necessary house supplies as you find you need for the kitchen and otherwise when I am up there on May 3d.

We also employed Ben Reno to paint the boats and to paint the metal work underneath the front porch. I will send up a metal brush and some paint, this week, so that he can get at it by the time he gets the boats finished, and it will be satisfactory for you to pay Ben such amount as you work out as fair for his work, and we will reimburse you when I am up there May 3d.

We want both of you to feel that the Vanderbilt Club is your home, and we want you to be happy and like it there, and the members want to do everything possible to make things agreeable for you. We know Mrs. Dud is an excellent cook, and we were delighted with the start we had with you last Saturday night for dinner.

On the other hand, when the members come to the Club they expect a lot of service, expect things neat and clean, and we believe we already know you well enough to feel that we are going to be happier than we have ever been before, with you in charge.

This is a long letter, but it is always good business to have things in writing, so that all of us know right where we stand before we start.

MOTOR WHEEL CORPORATION

SHEET NO. 4.

Mr. and Mrs. Vern Dud
4-22-29

As I told you Saturday, we hope that you have moved into the Vanderbilt Club to stay several years.

Very truly yours,

Carlton

CCCarlton:B

CCs to Messrs. C. M. Day
               J. B. Siegfried
               D. L. Porter
               W. C. Brock

MOTOR WHEEL CORPORATION

LANSING, MICHIGAN

OFFICE OF THE SECRETARY

December 21, 1929

Mr. and Mrs. Vernon Dudd,
Vanderbilt Club,
Vanderbilt, Michigan.

Dear Vern and Olga:

The members of the Vanderbilt Club want to express their appreciation for the excellent, efficient service, which you have rendered the Club and the individual members this year. Even more important than this, we wish to express our appreciation of the pleasant and happy way in which all of our affairs have been conducted.

The members of the Vanderbilt Club are really a hard working bunch and when they get to the Club, they want service but they appreciate more than anything else happiness, freedom from small petty troubles and worries.

And so we have greatly appreciated you and Peggy during the past year and now that Olga, Junior has been added to our family, we are happier than ever and we want you to know it and hope that you have been and will be equally happy with us.

Will you please accept the attached as a little expression of all that we have tried

-2-

to say above?

CCCarlton:A

Sincerely,

Carlton

For All Members of
The Vanderbilt Club

Treatment Regulator Corporation
GENERAL MOTORS BUILDING
DETROIT, MICH.

December 1, 1934

Mrs. Veron Dudd
Vanderbilt Club
Vanderbilt, Mich.

Dear Mrs. Dudd:

Please pardon the delay in replying to your letter, but it was necessary for me to go to Jackson to look up the Club records in order to answer you intelligently.

I have been located in Detroit for the past several months - in fact, the whole family is living here for the winter. The Club records were left in Jackson, and it has been rather awkward to take care of a lot of my personal affairs, being in Jackson so little.

I was there yesterday, and in looking over the Club books, found that the last wage check sent you was for September. I am enclosing check due you October 15th. This leaves the November 15th still unpaid.

The boys have been very slow in making their payments to the Club; in fact, Brock, Carlton and myself are the only ones that are up to date. I am communicating with the rest immediately, and will send you the November wage check just as soon as possible, which I am quite certain will not be many days.

It has been very disappointing to us that we have not been able to get up to the Club for the last two years. We thought surely we could have a re-union of the Scandinavian Evening. The Andersons and ourselves have mentioned and tentatively arranged this re-union many times, but something interfered on each occasion. We will all try to do better next year.

Sincerely,

Clarence M. Day/LH
(encl.)

MOTOR WHEEL CORPORATION

LANSING, MICHIGAN
February 12, 1936
(Dict. 2-11)

Mr. Vern Dudd
C/o Vanderbilt Club
Vanderbilt, Michigan

Dear Vern:

I am still wondering how you wrote a letter on February 2d and got it mailed so that it arrived in Lansing this morning. The snow is constantly increasing here and we have been having weather running from 13 below to three above, a high point, this morning. I know all the boys will appreciate your letter of the 2d and they will all read it.

As I remember it the lighting plant at the Lansing Club is a Delco plant. If you would be real still about it and not say anything about it around there I might be able to buy one of these from the factory at a very substantial discount and I hope I can convince the rest of the boys to go through with it.

The first thing I want to know is whether or not we have to buy any additional batteries? I can buy the entire plant, less batteries, very cheap. Before I do anything please let me know about that.

The boys will appreciate your suggestion about the addition and it is funny but I have thought about exactly the same thing a number of times. It would not only give us additional room but would make a fine cool place for the hot summer days. I don't suppose the boys would want to spend the money but I am letting them all read your letter.

I am sending along your fishing and weather and water reports to the boys which I found very interesting, not only because of the outside temperatures but also because of the water temperatures and, of course, I enjoyed the story about the fish swalling the theromometer which certainly has Ralph Hagamier stopped.

You probably have not heard of the terrible shock that Mrs. Carlton and I had last Friday morning and it is easier just to enclose a copy of letter I have written to my mother's nurse which tells you about all that I

-2-
Mr. Vern Dudd
Vanderbilt Club, Vanderbilt
2-12-36

can say.

Please accept the kindest regards and best wishes
for yourself, Mrs. Dudd and the girls.

                                    Sincerely yours,

                                    CCCarlton

COCarlton:C

MOTOR WHEEL CORPORATION

LANSING, MICHIGAN

June 15, 1937

Mr. and Mrs. Vern Dudd
Vanderbilt, Michigan

Dear Vern and Olga:

At a meeting of the boys of the Vanderbilt Club on June 9th the following was unanimously voted:

1. Effective June 10th we are to pay you $2.50 per day for meals. In case of anything less than a full day meals are to be divided as follows:

Breakfast	$.75
Lunch	.50
Dinner	1.25

2. Effective May 1, 1937, for the year following we will pay you $1,000, payable $83.33 monthly.

You will be glad to know that the unanimous feeling of the members is that we are very fortunate to have you running our club and we are glad to make the above increase to you as a token of our appreciation, realizing at the same time that the cost of living has increased.

Mr. Porter is today sending you a check to make up the difference between your former monthly payments and the above. You will also note that the increase in the price of meals is effective June 10th and therefore includes the Chrysler crowd that Frank Reinhart had up last week-end.

Sincerely yours,
CCCarlton

CCCarlton:M

CLARENCE M. DAY
~~XXXXXXXXXXXXXXXXXXXXXXXXXX~~
~~XXXXXXXXXXXX~~

11-204 General Motors Bldg.
Detroit, Michigan

October 7, 1937

Mr. and Mrs. Vernon Dadd
Vanderbilt Club
Vanderbilt, Michigan

Dear Folks:

I have talked with Larry Shaffner over the 'phone since his return, but have not had an opportunity of visiting with him.

From what he said, the boys all had a marvelous time at the Club, and certainly spoke nicely of you folks, which makes it very evident that you both added considerably to the enjoyment of their trip.

Larry had formed certain impressions of what the Club was, but after seeing it, he had very much under-estimated just what we had at Vanderbilt.

I wish to personally thank both of your for making the boys' trip as enjoyable as it was, and I am only sorry that the other three that had anticipated being there could not make it.

With kindest regards to both of you and the children, I am

Very sincerely yours,

Clarence M. Day/LH

Rockafellow
Grain and Seed Co.

BUSINESS ESTABLISHED 1887

ELEVATORS AT
CARSON CITY
VICKERYVILLE
MIDDLETON
ASHLEY

GENERAL OFFICE
CARSON CITY
MICH.

FIELD SEEDS, GRAIN, BEANS

Carson City Aug 15 1938

Mr and Mrs Leon Dudd
Vanderbilt Mich

Dear Mr and Mrs Dudd: Please accept my sincere thanks for the courtesy extended me during my pleasant week end visit at the Club. Your untiring efforts to provide for my comfort were very much appreciated.

Sincerely
Art Goulet

MOTOR WHEEL CORPORATION

LANSING, MICHIGAN

March 25, 1943

Mr. and Mrs. Vern Dudd
Vanderbilt Club
Vanderbilt, Michigan

Dear Vern and Olga:

    Your very interesting letter of the 24th was on my desk when I returned this morning from one of my rush-around trips. In fact it is so interesting that I am having copies made and mailing them to each member of the Club.

    I wish that I could take a look at that country while all the snow is still there, but that will be impossible. So first let's talk about what we can do to the Club.

    As I remember it, the season opens Saturday, April 24th. It certainly is going to be a late Spring, and consequently I haven't much desire to get up there that early.

    We don't know how we are going to get there at all, but somehow it's going to happen. I don't know whether we would dare attempt to drive up, and it makes me sick every time I think about trying to take a bus. The only comfortable way we can get there is to leave here at two o'clock in the afternoon and go to Detroit, and then take the sleeper, and it certainly is a mess to think of spending all that time to get to Vanderbilt when we have driven it so many times in four hours. You can't drive it in less than six hours now, and you really have to count on seven.

    I would much rather wait until the first or even the second Saturday in May, because when I come I want to stay a little longer than just a week-end.

    Anyway, it's too early now to think about it or make any definite plans, but I am sure there will be no one there April 24th, and I wouldn't worry a bit about early housecleaning.

    I think about all we want to do is clean up and spend no money unless there is some small thing that you know should be handled.

    In two or three weeks you will probably be able to get out to the Club again, and know what the wood situation is. I don't know how much was left from last Fall, and we shall have to have plenty of wood even if we don't come until the second Saturday in May.

MOTOR WHEEL CORPORATION

Mr. and Mrs. Vern Dudd

SHEET NO. 2
3/25/43

    Drop me another line when you are able to get out and take a look and of course I'll have it constantly in mind because I am just as anxious as ever to spend a few days there.

    Thanks for your fine letter.

    With kind regards and best wishes, and give Patty a big hug for me.

                                    Sincerely yours,

                                    C. C. CARLTON

CCC:R

BLACK STAR COAL CORPORATION
INCORPORATED
MINES AT ALVA, HARLAN COUNTY, KY.
TELEGRAPH, PINEVILLE, KY.
Sales Office: 303 Speed Building, Louisville, Ky.

ALVA, KENTUCKY
July 1st, 1943

Mr Verne Dudd,
Vanderbilt Lodge,
Vanderbilt Michigan.

Dear Verne:-

      You and Mrs Dudd were so swell to us, so thoughtful in every way to make our stay an enjoyable one, I'm taking this opportunity, even before getting back to work, to thank you both for just about the most enjoyable long week end, I have spent in many days.

      The rather trying situation existing in the coal industry, made my trip up most uncertain. Fortunately it all worked out for the best, I made the trip and I sincerely believe, had the best time of all. I havent laughed so heartily nor so continously in a long long time.

      The whole atmosphere of the lodge, the attractiveness of the lodge itself, the well kept grounds, that beautiful stream, those meals---yes those meals. Its the first time I have felt like eating 'fish fin feathers and all'. Its all due to you and Mrs Dudd, and this Southerner really had a great time being a visitor with you.

      With personal regards, and hoping to again be with you - someday- I am, with best wishes,

Sincerely yours

Albert B. Hill
Vice President

ABH/w

ROBERT GAGE COAL COMPANY
BAY CITY, MICHIGAN

JOHN A. CORYELL
VICE PRESIDENT

July 6, 1943.

Mr. Vern Dudd,
c/o Vanderbilt Club,
Vanderbilt, Mich.

Dear Vern:

    Enclosed please find my check for $57.75, for meals during the time that Bert Bean was up there.

    They had a good time, and spoke very highly of the meals you people got up for them.

    With best regards to Mrs. Dudd and yourself, I remain

                      Yours truly,

                        John A. Coryell

JAC.K

The Michigan Fertilizer Company
Wolverine Brands
PLANTS: LANSING, MICHIGAN
    CARO, MICHIGAN
Lansing, Michigan

LANSING
FACTORY AND OFFICE
HIGHMOUNT STREET
P. O. BOX 37

CARO PHONE 420
LANSING PHONE 2-1476

January 10, 1944

Mr. H. V. Dudd
Vanderbilt Club
Vanderbilt, Michigan

Dear Vern:

I received the dry cell batteries "okay", and these will help us out very much.

We rather looked for you folks to drop in around Christmas time -- did you come down this year?

We would like to do something around the Club next year toward the betterment of deer-hunting, etc. While it is too late this year to feed any hay, we definitely do want to prepare for feeding the deer next winter. We could send in a truck load of baled hay in the summer time and place this in such a position -- high enough off the ground so the deer would be assured of some feed furing the heavy snow.

Now, Vern, how about planting some rutabaga and carrot seed thruout the woods in the spring. If I get this seed, will you see that it is planted?

I was with Mr. Sprow this last week, and he asked about you folks -- I know he would enjoy hearing from you.

All the boys had a swell time this year, and I feel that next year will be even better so let's try and "boot" the hunting possibilities.

Let us hear from you.

Yours very truly,

Howard Fisher

H. C. FISHER

HCF/ek

COMMITTEE FOR ECONOMIC DEVELOPMENT
407 FISHER BLDG., DETROIT 2, MICH.

May 2, 1945

STATE CHAIRMAN
C. C. Carlton, V.P.-Sec'y,
Motor Wheel Corporation,
Lansing

STATE MANAGER
Edward C. Fielder
407 Fisher Bldg.,
Detroit 2

DISTRICT CHAIRMEN

District No. 1
H. Lynn Pierson, Pres.,
Detroit Harvester Company,
Detroit

District No. 2
H. Randall Wickes, Pres.,
Wickes Brothers,
Saginaw

District No. 3
George MaDan,
Public Accountant,
Lansing

District No. 4
F. C. Bowers, Pres.,
U. S. Register Company,
Battle Creek

District No. 5
Harry M. Taliaferro, Pres.,
American Seating Company,
Grand Rapids

District No. 6
Harold E. Johnson, Vice Pres.,
Burwood Products Company,
Traverse City

District No. 7
J. Emmet Richards,
Editor and Publisher,
Alpena News,
Alpena

RESEARCH
Robert N. Crom,
School of Business
Administration,
University of Michigan,
Ann Arbor

W. B. Hurley, Staff Engineer,
Detroit Edison Company,
Detroit

Mr. Vernon Dudd
Vanderbilt Club
Vanderbilt, Michigan

Dear Vern':

I made arrangements yesterday with the Michigan Bell Telephone Company to send to the Vanderbilt Club a Detroit telephone book. There were two or three times when I was up there when I would liked to have looked up Detroit telephone numbers or addresses and I imagine there are times when some of the members would want to do the same thing; hence, the Detroit telephone book might come in handy.

I used three of the six coupons sent to me by Mr. Carlton. I am sending to you, attached, the three remaining coupons. Before starting for home, I had Ray put in eight gallons, giving him one 5-gallon coupon -- the additional three gallons were charged to your account. I had previously used nineteen gallons of your surplus and with the three gallons, makes a total of twenty-two gallons. Deducting fifteen gallons, covered by the enclosed coupons, leaves a deficit of seven gallons.

Mrs. Fielder mentioned on the card she mailed you that we had a blow-out coming into Clare. Fortunately, it happened about a block from a Service Station. I was able to buy a recap and tube. We had our dinner while they were changing tires and when we returned, the car was all ready to start rolling again. If we had to have a blow-out, thank goodness, it happened just where it did and not out on the state road.

Yesterday being your birthday, we thought of you and hope that you did something a little different from the general routine so the day would be enjoyable to you.

I find being back in the harness is vastly different than complete relaxation in front of a crackling fire-place. The two weeks at the Lodge did me a tremendous amount of good. Mrs. Fielder likewise feels rested and "in the pink".

COMMITTEE FOR ECONOMIC DEVELOPMENT

Mr. Vernon Dudd   -2-

We reiterate our deep appreciation of the splendid manner in which the Dudd family took care of us.

Sincerely yours,

Edward C. Fielder

ECF:hk

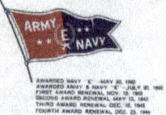

MOTOR WHEEL CORPORATION

LANSING 3, MICHIGAN

August 30, 1945

Mr. & Mrs. Vern Dudd
c/o Vanderbilt Club
Vanderbilt, Michigan

Dear Dudds:

    I regret that I have not sooner acknowledged your note attached to my bill but found my desk so full that I have just got around to handle things.

    We had an easy trip home and tried a new way, leaving 27 at Pruddenville taking 18 from there to Skeels and county gravel road from there to St. Louis which was a very good road except for the dust. For your information, would advise that in taking this route we made the trip from the club to Lansing, 199 miles.

    We found both of the dogs in good condition but very glad to get back home where they could run again.

    We want to take this opportunity to tell you how nice the club looked and what a very enjoyable time all of us had while we were there. I am inclosing my check for $126.39 in payment of your bill.

    I have today sent check to H. C. Walker, Gaylord, Michigan in amount of $83.28 in payment of furniture which I bought from them and am donating to the Vanderbilt Club. So that you may have the information for your inventory records that you are making up, would advise that their bill showed the following:

3 Tables	@	$ 9.50	$ 28.50
3 Lamps	@	7.95	23.85
3 Chairs	@	9.50	28.50
	Total		$ 80.85
	3% Tax		2.43
	Total		$ 83.28

MOTOR WHEEL CORPORATION

SHEET NO. 2

       I have discussed with Mr. Carlton and Mr. Holden relative to the wiring of these lamps on the partitions. It was decided that you had better get King out there and have him do away with the ceiling lights in the bedrooms, and have him run the two lines down to the top of the partition and down each side for a plug-in socket. In the single bedroom, discontinue the ceiling light and run that wiring down to the partition and put a socket at the bottom of the partition. This will then leave the two hall lights which turn on at the bottom of the stairs and also upstairs on a circuit by themselves, the same as they have been in the past.

       As to the cabinets, the one in the bedroom and the one on the front porch, I am taking the matter up with our Traffic Department to see if it is possible for us to send a truck up there to get same, but I am not sure that this can be done. Therefore, we would ask that Vern please see if any arrangements can be made with some trucking company to pick them up and deliver same to our Plant No. 1, Receiving Room, here and if so, approximate expense attached thereto.

       Again thanking you for all favors which you did for us and with kindest regards to all three Dudds from Mrs. Porter and myself, I beg to remain,

                                    Cordially yours,

Dic.:D.L.Porter
tl
Encl.

Black Star Coal Corporation
Incorporated
SPEED BUILDING » PHONE, JACKSON 4255 » LOUISVILLE, KENTUCKY

July 2, 1945

Personal

Mr. and Mrs. Verne Dudd
c/o Vanderbilt Club
Vanderbilt, Michigan

My dear Verne and Mrs. Dudd:

    Just a note to thank you again for your kindness and consideration during my visit last week with the rest of the gang to the Vanderbilt Club. You were both mighty fine and gracious in so many ways and contributed so much to a really pleasant visit and I want you to know that I am very grateful indeed. Each time I make this trip with Bert Bean and the rest of the fellows, it seems that we have more fun than ever and it is something that I always look forward to each year.

    Again thanking you and with my kind personal regards, I am,

Very sincerely yours,

T. E. Coleman

TEC:PO

MOTOR WHEEL CORPORATION

LANSING 3, MICHIGAN
September 9, 1946

Mr. H. Vern Dudd
℅ Vanderbilt Club
Vanderbilt, Michigan

Dear Vern:

Enclosed please find two checks made payable to you:

1. Check for $150.00 which we are sending to you to be used in payment of 10 cords of wood at $150.00 per cord. In the event that you are able to secure an additional 10 cords of wood, or whatever cords you can secure up to 10, if you will advise the writer accordingly we will send you check to cover whatever this additional amount is on the basis of $15.00 per cord.

2. We are inclosing check in amount $1,000.00 which we would ask that you please deposit in your bank as a special account and not in any way to be mixed up with your checking account. This account to be used wholly for the payment of all bills which you pay on account of the alterations and additions to present Vanderbilt Club Building and the new garage.

In issuing checks against this special account, you will please secure from the contractor or whoever has rendered you bill for work or material, and make notation on such bill as to the date paid, your check number and the amount of the check. As fast as these bills are paid by your use of this special account, you will please forward bills to me at once so that we may know how your funds in this special account stand and when it will be necessary to send you additional funds.

We, of course, from the fact that you issued check on this special account in payment of the bill rendered, must of necessity assume that you know same to be correct and if for material that the material has been delivered and if for labor that you assume that the contractor is just in his charges.

This may seem a little out of the ordinary but it is very essential that we keep all costs that go into the property account.

MOTOR WHEEL CORPORATION

Mr. H. Vern Dudd   SHEET NO. 2
                                              9/9/46

       If there are any questions that you may have relative to this subject, please advise. Also advise the name of the bank and the title of the account. Perhaps it might be well to open this as a joint account between Mrs. Dudd and yourself with both of your signatures on record for the withdrawal of funds from the account so that if the occasion should arise and you would not be available, Mrs. Dudd could issue check to cover.

                               Yours very truly,

                               D. L. Porter

DLP:tl
Encl.

The number of letters Grandma saved slowed down, considerably, by December of 1949. The saved letters stop all together with the passing of C.C. Carlton in June of 1951.

CLARENCE C. CARLTON
Heart attack fatal

C. C. Carlton, Wheel Firm Official, Dies

LANSING—(AP)—Clarence C. Carlton, 69, vice president and secretary of the Motor Wheel Corp., died Saturday of a heart ailment.

Mr. Carlton served as a member of the Automotive Council for War Production in World War II.

A native of Akron, O., Mr. Carlton attended the universities of Akron, Michigan and Chicago. He served as superintendent of schools at Mantua and Medina, O., before becoming secretary to the president of the Firestone Tire & Rubber Co. in Akron in 1912.

* * *

MR. CARLTON moved to Lansing in 1917 to become sales manager of the Prudden Wheel Co., later merged with the Auto Wheel Co. to form the Motor Wheel Corp.

With the merger in 1920 he became secretary of the wheel company and was made vice president in 1938.

Surviving are his wife, Emily E., and two sons, Thomas R. Carlton, of Santa Ana, Calif., and James C. Carlton, of Philadelphia.

Over the years, Mom entertained us with many stories about her childhood in the Pigeon River Forest and growing up in the woods. In the summer, her chores included taking care of Club members, cleaning the lodge, and helping with meals.

She was excited when entire families would arrive … that meant kids to play with. The Holdens came with their three children. They said the northern air seemed to help with their daughter Patty's hay fever. The Carltons came many times. Mrs. Carlton gave Mom a custom-made English bamboo 3 ¾ ounce fly rod, reel, leaders, and fly box that was owned by her daughter, Emily (my sister Becky still has the rod). Mom's bike had belonged to the Carltons' daughter, Janet, and Mom's constant four-legged companions, Duffy and Toffee, were given to her by the Carltons, AKC papers included. The Carltons lived in Lansing and, years later, would check in on Mom when she attended Michigan Agricultural College.

> *Interestingly, in all my years, I never saw Mom pick up her special 3 wt. bamboo fly rod, or any rod, and toss around her favorite Royal Coachman dry fly she talked about so often. She talked about this activity of her youth all the time, but I never witnessed it in my lifetime. Mom seemed much more content to focus on important ancillary topics. She spoke of the "environs where trout are found," (John Voelker, The Testament of a Fisherman) and the thoughts, memories, places, and people that occupied her sport. This was what she (and Dad), over the years, would stuff into the many pockets of our fishing vests and it was all bound to this past time just as tightly as the guides were wrapped to our fly rods. There was much more to fly fishing than fly fishing, at least that seemed to be her ultimate message—mission accomplished! None of us kids ever joined the ranks of the highly accomplished fly fishermen or the true trout bum. We all viewed fly fishing as a package deal. The anticipation and preparation for a trip and the memories generated after seemed more important than the actual moment of engagement. We would quickly forget our fish count, but we never forgot the people, places, events, good meals, and conversations. Years later, Dad's heart surgery almost derailed one of our yearly fly fishing trips. The surgeon insisted Dad take it easy for several days when he got home. We asked him*

what he meant by home. After we straightened that out, we picked Dad up from the hospital, got his new medications, and headed directly to fish camp. We all stayed inside with him, until he got his strength back and finally got in the water five days later. It didn't seem right to get in the water without him—a package deal.

Young guests and Mom (center) with a nice day's catch

"Peggy and I with the two cocker spaniels that Mr. Carlton gave me. Duffy is by Peggy and Toffee is by my feet." – Mom

"Me and dog Duffy" - Mom

"I believe I must have spent most of my time on my bike—a Schwinn given to me by Mr. Carlton. The bike was his daughter Janet's." - Mom

Their family's modest monthly income did not leave a lot for extras. Living in relative isolation most of the year offered little opportunity to see the outside world. Mom spoke of very few people or locations, other than Club guests and maybe trips to town for supplies. She only spoke of frequent local visitors, Harry and Charley.

Mom always talked about her bike—she would occasionally ride it off the Club property onto Old Vanderbilt Road. When a rare, approaching car could be heard coming down the dirt road, she quickly rode her bike off the road and hid in the ferns. She reemerged after the car had safely passed. She never did quite explain why she did this.

"So it was very special for just Mom to take her yearly excursion with Mrs. Carlton back to Lansing for the weekend. Mom looked forward to the trip all year long. Quite often this would be the only large city Mom would see for the entire year. Regular supply trips to Vanderbilt and occasional excursions to Gaylord pretty much summed up the rest of her yearly travels. This one trip to Lansing was special. It was at this time Mrs. Carlton would take Mom shopping. She always bought Mom a new winter coat and more. She would also gather up her daughter's previous winter and summer clothes and send this home with Mom. Her daughter was about the same size as Mom and she never wore clothes for more than one season. These hand me downs fit just fine. When she arrived home, she had a totally new wardrobe. She could wear all her new clothes and coat to school without fearing that anybody had ever seen the clothes before. The next summer when Emily returned to the Club with her parents, Mom would begin to get an idea what her next year's wardrobe would look like."

Pete Mutch memo, written late 1990s

"Harry and me on our bikes" – Mom

Mom spoke many times about Harry and Charley. They would drop by the Club to visit or lend a helping hand. Mom recalled that "Harry lived in a one-room shack through the pines on the south off White House Trail Road. He smelled and was dirty. He hunted, trapped, and grew a beautiful garden." Shortly after Mom graduated from high school, Harry moved into Vanderbilt and lived upstairs in the old jail. He even wrote Mom several letters after Mom left for college. Mom recalls that Harry died in the fire when the jail burned. Charley was the caretaker for the Young property that went from the Iron Bridge over the Pigeon River on Old Vanderbilt Road downstream to the "Meadows," not far upstream from the Club property.

"Harry by the river" – Mom

"Harry Karslake worked for Mr. Higgins and lived in a shack beyond the pines on White House Trail Road. He was a raggedy man. He worked for Pa, the goodest man you ever saw." – Mom

"Charlie Forbes lived by the iron bridge that crosses the Pigeon shortly before you get to Hoobler's Road. He was the caretaker for the Young property. He and Harry were buddies when they were speaking to each other." – Mom

In Mom's free time, she and Grandpa Dudd would catch "muddlers" during the day and use them to catch the "big trout" from the wooden footbridge at night. One trout was so big that they yelled for Grandma's help. She waded into the river and cradled the fish in the apron she was wearing. When she placed it in the old laundry tub, it curled up on both ends.

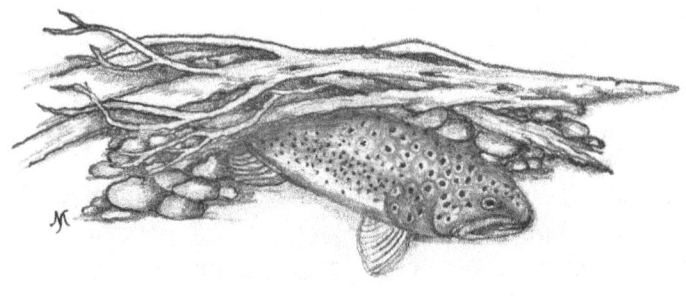

Big trout under the bridge

We always laughed when Mom told us the story about dropping Grandpa's new hammer down the hole in the outhouse and how sister Peggy held on to Mom as she reached down to retrieve it.

An actual event mixed with some embellishment—the Club had indoor plumbing and the outhouse was no longer in use when mom lived there.

"Going shopping for anything other than supplies was a bit unusual. Sure, Grandpa had an open charge account with the local stores—all three of them. But you didn't buy anything you couldn't justify. The monthly statements were sent to the Club treasurer for their perusal and payment. Grandpa was never questioned about his purchases, and was very careful not to abuse this trust. On one occasion he felt the need to buy a new hammer. Mom said he was so proud of his new purchase that he smiled for weeks. Little did he know that his Stanley was almost lost for good shortly after it arrived home. Well, I guess I shouldn't say lost. Mom and sister Peggy knew where it was, they weren't sure they could get it back. That day Mom and Peggy were making repairs to their dollhouse. As usual the door was open to allow light in and, more importantly, to keep a constant flow of fresh air circulating. No sooner had they begun to use the hammer when it slipped. Down through one of the two plate sized dark holes, cut into the bench at the back of the dollhouse, it fell. Instant panic set in. Mom knew all too well what surprises lurked down there. In addition, time was a factor. The dollhouse welcomed visitors throughout the night and day and more calling cards would only obscure the exact location of the hammer. So, with stealth like mission, they ran to the garage where they found rope and a flashlight. With childhood innocence, Mom approached Grandpa asking if he could tie a slip knot. The kids were relieved that he asked no questions. They ran back to the dollhouse where their strategy was finalized. Peggy, eight years older and bigger, would lower Mom through the hole with the slip knot tied around her ankles. Mom remembers the hard part was just getting her shoulders through the hole. Once through, she turned on the flashlight.

Suddenly, a whole new world appeared. She quickly located the hammer, as it had come to rest on one of the many Sears Catalog pages. Peggy then pulled Mom back through the hole and the mission was completed. They took the hammer down to the river, cleaned it up a bit, and replaced it in Grandpa's tool box. He never did find out where his hammer had been that day and Mom never told him."

Pete Mutch short story, written late 1990s

Outhouse

Grandma, although not teaching at the time, was an educator and kept Mom current with her studies until she started school at Vanderbilt in second grade. On Sundays, during the winter, Mom and Peggy would walk or snowshoe the "Grade" to Sturgeon Valley Road where people from Vanderbilt would pick them up and they'd board in town for the school week.

Grade Road was once an old railroad grade used for logging. This short stretch of road connected Old Vanderbilt Road to Sturgeon Valley Road. My early recollection of the grade was a dusty dirt road, cutover and treeless on both sides with the exception of two stately red pines to the west that we called Jack and Jill. On Friday, the girls were driven back to where they could walk the remaining distance home.

When the school bus could make it to the Club, the bus driver and the girls would be on the lookout for "Pete," the blind elk. The bus came to a total stop when Pete was in the middle of the narrow dirt road. One of the kids on the bus would take an apple from their lunch pail and lead blind Pete to the side of the road so the bus could keep moving. By the late 1970s, Grade Road had become Dudd Road.

> *Elk disappeared from Michigan in the late 19th century due to unrestricted hunting and loss of their habitat. In 1918, seven Rocky Mountain elk were brought to the area that would soon be the Pigeon River Forest. The herd grew steadily, but poaching and diminished habitat quality reduced its numbers from 1,500 in the early 1960s to 200 in the mid-1970s. Since then, careful management of the open areas and forests that the herd needs to thrive has helped it grow to more than 1,100 animals.*
>
> *My North News Service, July 15, 2019*

ELK IN THE PIGEON RIVER COUNTRY

It takes big country to support big animals.

Between 1916 and 1918, there were at least 3 attempts to release Rocky Mountain Elk in northern Michigan in an effort to replace the native Eastern Elk that disappeared by 1900.

Their release was part of a growing conservation movement to create game preserves and recreation areas on burnt-over lands.

The 7 or 8 elk released in Cheboygan County in 1918 successfully established themselves and became the foundation of today's herd of more than 1,100 animals.

Elk release

The closest family around was the Horsells. Mr. Horsell was the superintendent of Pigeon River Forest from 1923 to 1952. He lived at the DNR Headquarters with his wife and seven kids. Mom remembers having dinners with the Horsells and eating at the long dining room table in the old DNR Headquarters building—now the newly opened Pigeon River Country Discovery Center.

I spoke with his son, Lyle, about his early Pigeon River memories, the Vanderbilt Club, and Mom. He graduated from Vanderbilt High School in 1948 with Mom and seven other classmates. Mom, Shirley MacGregir, and Lyle were the original three classmates, together since early elementary school. Other kids were added over the years, so the graduating class of nine was Patty Dudd, Shirley MacGregir, Lyle Horsell, Blanch Sides, Ruth Miller, Thelma Lamb, Evelyn Smith, Ronald Smith, and Richard Sides.

Lyle was class president and picked a nice day around the first of May for their senior class skip day. All nine of the classmates fit into one car and drove to the Soo (Sault Saint Marie, Michigan). They spent the day watching boats going through the locks.

They raised money for their senior class trip by putting on plays, dances, and other events. After graduation, they went on their senior trip to Niagara Falls, New York City, and Washington, DC. They took two cars. Their class sponsor, a teacher, drove one car and the girls' chaperone drove the other. Two classmates couldn't make the trip, so a total of nine set out on a one-week trip.

Lyle worked for the DNR in high school and left for the Navy after graduation. He then spent forty years with Ford Motor Company, mostly in Dearborn, and finally returned to Gaylord seven years ago.

His older brother, Bill, worked for the DNR fisheries division. Bill would later marry Mom's classmate, Ruth Miller. As you might recall, it was Bill and Ruth who asked Mom, Dad, Nan, my boys and me to attend the Elkland Seniors luncheon where we met Ken Mudget. That chance meeting deserves some of the credit for this book.

Vanderbilt High School class of 1948. Mom outlined in the bottom left corner.

Mom's fiftieth Vanderbilt High School class reunion

"The log building that now houses the Pigeon River Country Discovery Center was built in 1935 by the Civilian Conservation Corps as a home for forester William Horsell, his wife, and seven children. It has been described as the best, and best preserved, example of CCC architecture in Michigan." — Photo courtesy of Pigeon River Country Discovery Center

Mom (and Dad) spent the better part of their winter in 2010 putting together a much-treasured photo album of her time at the Vanderbilt Club. She placed a caption under each picture. These photos and many others like them helped lend great visual support to the many stories she told me over my lifetime.

"The way the Club looked when I called it home. Taken from the bridge." – Mom
You can see the old, original outhouse on the extreme left, and Mom's sleeping quarters (her house) on the right facing toward the bridge. "Mom's house" had just enough room for two twin beds, two desks, a wood stove, and a Victrola.

"The cabin (my house) where Peg and I slept" – Mom

"Back view of the Club looking upstream" – Mom

"Me in swing by clothesline, the old barn in the background" – Mom

"The engine house. Our electricity was generated here—a Chrysler engine and storage batteries filled the inside. 32 volt DC power was generated and required a converter for anything that was 110 volt AC." – Mom

"Some Club members near engine house with Dad (in foreground)" – Mom

"Murray D. Van Wagoner, a guest at the Club. He was governor of Michigan and served on the Mackinac Bridge Authority." – Mom

"Peg and I near my birthday tree planted the fall of 1929—a Norway. Garage in background" – Mom

"It dawned on me as we neared the completion of this project that I hadn't included any pictures of Mother, probably because she was always working while I rode my bike and fished. Not true. I can remember doing a lot of work as a kid, always dishes and cleaning, a habit that still sticks with me. I love to clean. This picture is of Mom on the left, Sally next, Sally's Mom (guests at the Club, from Ohio), and Jeanne Thorsen (Marion's daughter)." – Mom

Mom lived the entire year at the Club until Grandpa and Grandma moved the family into the town of Vanderbilt for the winters beginning in 1941. They stayed in their aluminum trailer parked behind the meat market. Peggy had graduated a year earlier and left Vanderbilt to pursue a career in nursing and Mom was entering junior high. Once in town for the winter, Grandma returned to teaching kindergarten. Grandpa ran the Vanderbilt Ski Club for Mort Neff. In the spring, as the school year concluded and the ski hill closed for the season, they moved back to the Club. According to the Otsego Chamber of Commerce 50th Anniversary History:

> The Vanderbilt Ski Club was a predecessor to the Otsego Ski Club at nearby Gaylord (opened in 1939), this area used steel wheels from Ford Model A's as pulleys for the rope tows. The Vanderbilt Ski Club was located at Cherwinski Rd. at Old

Vanderbilt Rd. On Friday, March 14, 1941, in an article about winter sports in Michigan, the Cass City Chronicle listed among seven ski areas in lower Michigan:

– *The Vanderbilt Ski Club, with its superb, breath-taking thrill of a 1,400-foot run in a sheer 18 seconds' time*

Grandpa Dudd

Mom, Grandma and Grandpa

Mom always said Grandpa worked for Mort Neff at the Vanderbilt Ski Club. A group of five (some records indicated six) Detroit businessmen, led by Don McLouth, president at the McLouth Steel Corporation, bought the property in 1936. McLouth also owned Green Timbers, over six thousand acres of private hunting and fishing property that was eventually added to the Pigeon River Forest. Vanderbilt was quite an active little town when wealthy people came by train from the cities to enjoy the ski club. The partners eventually decided to move their ski club operation to Gaylord, just down the road, because they needed more property to expand. The Otsego

Ski Club, Hidden Valley, opened in 1942. I could not find any information that put Mort Neff in an investor or management position. Mort graduated in 1927 from the University of Michigan with a double major in journalism and electrical engineering. He began writing a small outdoor sports column for a Detroit newspaper. In 1942 he began a radio show and his television program, *Michigan Outdoors*, debuted in 1951 and ran for twenty-three straight years, the longest-running outdoor and sportsman show in American television history. Records indicate that he visited the ski club, but no mention of any involvement beyond that. One newspaper introduced Mortimer and his wife as being the Chrysler Group. The four letters Grandma saved seem to suggest that Mort was more than just a typical guest and that Mom was right—Grandpa did, in fact, work for Mort Neff.

My guess is that while Mort Neff was not an original owner of the Ski Club, he may have eventually acquired some ownership. Some sources have suggested that other partners were added beyond the original five or six to as many as nine. Mom always spoke of Mort Neff, Fred Booth and Don McLouth as owners and recalls these men would occasionally visit with Grandpa at the Vanderbilt Club.

VANDERBILT SKI CLUB
VANDERBILT
MICHIGAN

December 16th, 1941

Mr. Vernon Dudd,
Vanderbilt, Michigan.

My dear Vern:

We were all very much pleased by the amount of work accomplished last week end, and it is very gratifying to us to see the cooperation that is set up now between the club and you, Herman Berendt, and I hope, the whole town. Herman is a pretty foxey old boy, and certainly knows a lot about the mechanics required in setting up that tow. Also, I think he takes a great deal of personal satisfaction in working with you, and I hope you'll use him frequently.

The triple blocks have been shipped via prepaid express from Strollinger hardware today. I suggest you call me at home, Birmingham 915, collect, Thursday night at eleven o'clock. I'm afraid I won't be home until then. You can give me all the developments up to that time.

I trust that you have started building the cover for the new tow. Remember, that tow is not to be used until George Booth or I arrive to install the safety, and that will not be before December 26th or 27th at the earliest. However, by that time I expect the whole rig will be in running condition except for the finishing touches when we get there.

I talked/to Fenn Holden this morning and he said that he had discussed the method of taking up enough slack in the big tow rope so that you could get it around the snatch block shiv without any trouble. I hope you get the anchor post and dead man buried before too much frost gets in the ground. You and Mrs. Dudd have probably done the dish shopping and have got everything you need including the stove for the kitchen. I am ordering a small Duo Therm circulating heater to be put in the ladies room, and it will be shipped directly to you for proper installation.

As you know, we're going to have to take awfully good care of the tow ropes both on the big tow and the new little one. At the end of our skiing day, and possibly during the day, as temperature and weather conditions vary, we will have to release the tension as the rope becomes taut. It will be necessary to rig up a couple of "lazy y" sticks to hold the rope off the ground where there are not enough shiv posts.

Letters from Mort Neff. Grandma and Grandpa ran the Vanderbilt Ski Club for Mort Neff in the early 1940s.

VANDERBILT SKI CLUB
VANDERBILT
MICHIGAN

Page Two.

Send in any incidental bills, such as trucking the tow rope, at once. And speaking of finances, remember, we are a non-profit corporation, operating mighty close to a budget, so I'm trusting that you'll help keep our operating expense and costs down in so far as extra labor is concerned.

How do you want to be paid? George tells me your work began December 1st, and it will probably go well into March. Just let me know how you want this paid off as we go along.

I have no idea how many will be going north this weekend, and that makes it very difficult for you and Mrs. Dudd to plan food preparations. However, I doubt very much that there will be more than a dozen people there, if that many. There may not be any at all. I suggest you check with Marge Campbeill or Mrs. Berendt to see if they know of any guests making plans for this coming week-end. The big rush will come the week after Xmas, and by New Year's Eve, the town will be filled up. The entire following week-end will be the busiest of the season no doubt, and there will probably be upwards of 100 people on the hill from December 31st, thru Sunday the 4th.

I like your idea of preparing a variety of foods in town and taking them up to the hill and using our new cooking range to keep them warm and serve them piping hot. Don't forget to look over the toboggan in Letson's Ski shack, and see if you can patch it up to serve as a sled transport then dope out some kind of a hitch for the Tow rope and you'll be all set.

We are depending on you for weather reports. If anybody calls you, or if you write me with a general report on weather conditions, (and I think a post card a couple of times a week would be helpful) always report the condition on the hill itself rather than back in the woods or valleys. The information should reveal whether it's crusted, wet, dry-powder, or a combination, and of course the depth. Also note whether or not all grass and stubble is covered. George is worried about the drifts under the top tow. After these are cleared, either by hand or Mother Nature, we're afraid the drifting will continue and this would make it almost impossible to use the top tow at all. So, we're leaving this up to your good judgement to remxxedy. Keep me posted! We're mighty pleased with your work, and we have every confidence in presenting our members with the finest club management we've ever had.

VANDERBILT SKI CLUB
VANDERBILT
MICHIGAN

Page Three.

Best personal wishes,
Mort.

P. S. Tell Bill Nesbitt the $4.00 a day deal is okay.
Here's his check for two and a half days work put in last week-end. Please keep an account of his time and payments made.

NEFF RADIO PRODUCTIONS
DETROIT • RANDOLPH 3006

CLIENT_____
STATION_____
TIME_____

COPY

Vern:

    I have just finished talkimg to Gordon Karslake by phone. Dave Wallace and Fenn Holden --- head men on the tow -- have ordered the differential locked on the big motor. That's where the slipping has been taking place, and they want it locked, with no back lash, at once. Gordon probably has gotten in touch with you by now, and will need plenty of help in getting the differential out and down to the shop to work on. Give him every possible assistance, and have the unit assembled and the ropes back on the drums by the week end. Herman may help you.

    I'll bring up the fuel pump with me.

    For the time being the ropewill remain in one piece, until Wallace and Holden get the new drums on. Then we will cut it and run the upper and lower tows off the one motor, slipping one or the other rope off the drum when we don't need it. This means we will NOT get a new motor for the top.

    Hope you have Stanley on the job getting the new location for the little tow all set. Expect to hear from you tomorrow about that ½" rope at Audrain's, -- also the 1" stuff. I now have a line on 1200 feet of 1" rope just like we have and believe we will get it at once.

    And do something about getting more xxxx SNOW!!!

                                                          MORT

P.S. Everyone complimentary about the Dudd Management and cuisine, but don't let it go to your head. When shall I start giving you fishing lessons?

NEFF RADIO PRODUCTIONS
1305 STROH BUILDING
DETROIT

Monday

My dear Mrs. Dudd:

I was so disgusted with weather conditions Sunday that I didn't have a chance to tell you how sorry I was about all the trouble you had gone to for naught in preparing for Sunday's crowd.

Here is our check for $20.00 which I hope will be enough to cover the losses you have experienced in the two week ends on which the waether knocked all our plans upside down.

I think you realize that the snow conditions are not at all normal this year, and the experience you're having should be no guide for the future. I mention the future hopefully, because everyone, without exception, is enthusiastic about the way you and Vern have taken hold of things at the club, and if war permits skiing next year we'll want you on the job again.

After the season's over I'd like to have a complete report from you, with suggestions for next year.

I fully intended to take over your daughter for a little private instruction this past week end. It's wonderful to see her on skis, and we'll see to it that she gets plenty of help from all of us next week end....weather permitting!

Best personal wishes, and tell Vern I'll get a letter off to him later today, or tomorrow for sure.

Sincerely,
Mort Neff

*
RANDOLPH
3006

NEFF RADIO PRODUCTIONS
1305 STROH BUILDING
DETROIT

Wednesday

Dear Vern:

I'm back on the job again after a couple of days over in Chicago at the 6th Corps Area Headquarters. They've got my number, brother, and I'm having one heluva time trying to get better than a shavetail's rating!

Skiing hasn't been on my mind, and I'm sorry you've been neglected financially! Here's a batch of checks which my socretary says takes care of everything. There's a book-keepi error, however, resulting from that cash transaction with the tow money, paying Bill Nesbitt. As a result of this error your personal check for $91.88 is $23.25 too high.

In other words you have cash on hand in the amount of $23.25 with which to pay current bills as they are due. For our books, see that you have receipts for these payments, please. If there's any confusion in your mind about this let me know at once. The $11 tow money from lastweek end you can hold for me, for payment into the tow account. This helps keep our books straight.

Yep, my leg is in bad shape. Pulled muscle and plenty sore Wouldn't have minded it if I had done it skiing! Chances are I can't handle the boards this week end, but may bring Joey up anyway, and take some pictures.

Now all you have to do is keep the temperature reasonably low and hold onto that snow. I'm afraid we'd be taking an awful gamble in promoting another ski week at this late date. Long week ends might work, however. You didn't explain why a new splice is necessary in the little rope. A new break or did the old splice let go again?

Keep me posted on snow conditions....hope to see you Friday night. Will probably come on the bus. There'll be at least one special, maybe two, tell Mrs. Berndt.

RANDOLPH
3006

Chapter 2

At the time, many other hunting and fishing clubs, representing a wide variety of industries and professions, dotted the riverbanks of the Pigeon, Sturgeon, and Black. Even more clubs were established only a few miles south along the large Au Sable River system, beginning with the North Branch. Not only did the clubs provide an opportunity to relax with family and friends, but I suspect they cultivated and secured many business deals as well. The original hotel registry in the lobby of the Lovells Douglas House, on the banks of the North Branch of the Au Sable River, dated June 10, 1917, had weekend guests Henry and Edsel Ford. Grandpa's brother, Thurlow Dudd of Johannesburg, signed in the next day.

> *North Branch Outing Club (NBOC) was established by lumber baron T.E. Douglas after he realized his lumber business was on the decline. Douglas started promoting fly fishing on the North Branch of the Au Sable to prominent anglers of the time. Men and women anglers came from around the world to fly fish the North Branch of the Au Sable. NBOC had members and guests such as Henry and Edsel Ford, Harvey Firestone, the Dodge brothers, Thomas Edison, as well as royalty from Europe. The North Branch Outing Club was a true "Elite American" fly fishing destination. – NBOC website*

	Arnold Boutell	Saginaw
	Sunday June 10th 17	
	Henry Ford	Dearborn, M...
	Edsel B. Ford	Detroit
	Am X. Harting	"
	Ula Mae Shier	
	Vera Leone Shier	
	Chas. Abbott	
	Fred Martin	
	Mr & Mrs I. N. Hanson	Trufin
	Miss Virginia Hanson	"
	W. C. Manor	"
	H. A. Crecique	Grayling
	Mr Boyd & Family (3)	"
	Oscar Hanson	
	Rube Babbitt	

Douglas House hotel registry

Douglas House hotel registry

Douglas House

Early photo of
Grandpa Dudd (Vern)
with brothers Thurlow
and Clarence

These new visitors to the area stimulated a new economy that spawned hotels, river guides, Au Sable River boat makers, fly tiers, bamboo rod makers, and more. Entire books have been written about the area's lumber history; the concerned citizens who became involved in the conservation and sustainability issues that followed the aggressive lumbering; and the individuals who were attracted to these rivers and their contributions to our past and current fly fishing opportunities and regulations. Trout Unlimited, now a worldwide organization, got its origin in 1959 on the banks of the Au Sable River, under the inspiration of George Griffith, Art Neumann, and others.

According to Patrick Dunn in his piece, "The Big Wild," from May 26, 2020, in 1927, just two years before Mom was born and brought home to the Club, P.S. Lovejoy became the "state's first Game Division Chief and later Chief of Land Planning. … Lovejoy is credited with originally creating what he called the BIG Wild—the Pigeon River Country State Forest. He had a vision, which evolved out of the dissolution of the lumbering era, to pioneer new concepts of land management." Dave Smethurst best explained Lovejoy's wilderness concept: "A wilderness is a land that shows no evidence of being touched by man, and we, purposely back when we (Lovejoy) started all this, wanted the Pigeon River Country to be a working forest that gave the feeling of wilderness. In the Pigeon, if you walk for fifteen minutes, you can pretty much be alone. The Pigeon is a place for solitary recreation—the place to explore on your own."

I asked Lyle Horsell to give me a few other names he associated with the past and continued development of the Pigeon River Forest. First on his list was his dad, William H. Horsell, superintendent of the Pigeon River Forest from 1923 to 1952. Ford Kellum, Dave Smethurst, and Jerry Myers also came to mind. This trio of names came together in January 1972 to form the Pigeon River Country Association. Their immediate mission was to oppose the aggressive oil drilling that was about to completely change Lovejoy's wilderness concept. Oil drilling began on May 27, 1970. Oil companies were proposing to drill up to one thousand wells in this remote forest. These three men, along with other concerned citizens, helped create a workable plan that saved the forest we enjoy today.

Dale Franz's book, *Pigeon River Country*, is a must read for anybody wanting to learn more about the people and the Pigeon. In Franz's book, he points out how American journalist, novelist, and sportsman, Ernest Hemingway, passed by the front gate of the Vanderbilt Club, one hundred years ago, while on Old Vanderbilt Road, on his way to camp and fish on the Black River.

In a July 26, 1919, letter to a friend, Howell Jenkins, Hemingway talked fondly about the Pigeon River Country. He called it the Pine Barrons and said they could "nearly drive across" it "without any road just by compass. It is so free from under brush." He told Jenkins, "That Barrons Country is the greatest I've ever been in" and that "there are some great camping places on the Black." ... The road Hemingway traveled from Vanderbilt still exists as a narrow dirt road, closely lined by woods. It is now called Old Vanderbilt Road and runs parallel to the newer, paved Sturgeon Valley Road. ... Hemingway took the Vanderbilt Road again in August 1920 and camped at the Black River. He and four friends were gone for six days in a rented car with a trailer. ... "It was great in camp lying all rolled up in the blankets after the fire had died down to coals and the men were asleep and looking at the moon and thinking long, long thoughts." ... In October, Hemingway met Elizabeth Hadley Richardson, and by spring they planned to marry. On April 28 that year he wrote to Bill Smith that he would "sometimes get thinking about the Sturgeon and Black during the nocturnal [night] and damn near go cuckoo. ... May have to give it up for something I want more—but that doesn't keep me from loving it with everything I have. Dats de way things are. Guy loves a couple or three streams all his life and loves 'em better than anything in the world—falls in love with a girl and the goddam streams can dry up for all he cares. Only the hell of it is that all that country has had a bad hold on me as ever."

Pigeon River Country, *Dale Franz, 1976*

The Pigeon River Country had a profound effect on many people, including a young Bill Ford (eventual executive chairman of Ford Motor Company). In Zeigler's book, Ford says his environmental bent and efforts to address greenhouse gases at the corporate level "came from my love of the outdoors, which came from my love of fly fishing" (*Famous Fly Fishers*, Norm Zeigler, 2018). His early fly fishing years were spent with guide, mentor, and eventual lifelong friend, Walter Babcock. Bill enjoyed many worldwide fishing opportunities, "but if I had one day to spend it would be on a small river in northern Michigan." These formative fly fishing years were spent fishing with Babcock at the Fontinalis Club on the Sturgeon River (Club Stream) just outside of Vanderbilt. I asked Bill Ford about these early fishing memories. "Most of the time I spent in the Vanderbilt area has been at the Fontinalis Club, but my memories of Vanderbilt include fishing the Pigeon and previously owning a cabin on the Black River."

Today's Big Wild enthusiasts and supporters are many. The Pigeon River Country Association has a seat on the board of the Pigeon River Advisory Council which reports to the Michigan DNR, all established to better serve the forest. In 2019, the year before COVID-19, 37,521 vehicles entered the forest, an area half the size of New York City, to enjoy all the forest has to offer—fauna and flora, birding, fishing, hunting, hiking, equestrian opportunities, camping, and much more. The Pigeon River Discovery Center "Welcomes (you) to the Pigeon River Country. It's big, it's wild, and it's quiet. There's magic in it. Things happen here that happen nowhere else." Michigan artist and author, Gwen Frostic, would encourage us to embrace an area, such as the Pigeon River Forest, by simply enjoying its "symphony in silence."

> "Everyone came and marveled at the forest's greatness and natural beauty, its solitude and ruggedness—and then they went home—to an environment of conveniences, dependable warmth and income. The 'tives' as Grandma called them were those that stayed behind, year-round, and called this area home. This is where they made their living, raised their kids, and usually retired. There was a time, I'm sure, when Mom thought that front yards of trailing arbutus, lady slippers and sweet fern were nothing but mere weeds that failed to look anything like the yards found in town and down state. Back yards of pine and cedar, the Pigeon River, and the swamp that lay beyond

were, undoubtedly, uninspiring to a young child wishing for neighbors and playmates. And a small caretaker's cabin built from the woods that surrounded it with its outhouse located a short distance out the back door was probably a constant reminder of her humble existence. But this was home; this was the Vanderbilt Club in the 1930's and 1940's."

Pete Mutch memo, written late 1990s

Mom graduated from Vanderbilt High School in 1948 as the valedictorian in a class of nine. She went on to attend Michigan State College of Agriculture and Applied Science (renamed Michigan State University in 1964), where she met Dad on a blind date. "Just look for the girl in the red coat," he was told. Dad chuckles when he tells this story. When he got to the steps of the campus library, a bit of panic immediately set in. It appeared that red was a popular coat color that year. Dad, being the quiet and shy type, decided to wait it out until one of the red coats might finally approach him. Lucky for all of us, Mom finally made the first move.

Dad visited Mom at the Club in the summer between college terms. Years later when we asked what had attracted him to Mom, we jokingly suggested, "Maybe it was because Mom came with river frontage." When he visited, he slept on the big screened-in riverside porch and still recalls falling asleep to the sound of the river. Dad always loved to fly fish and even brought his Dad and best friends to fish the Club.

Dad's (right) early days at the Club

Grandpa Russel Mutch (right) and one of Dad's buddies at the Club

Chapter 3

Dad (Phil) was born on August 31, 1930, in West Branch, Michigan, and brought home to a farm his dad was managing in Lupton. His dad, my Grandpa Russell Mutch, the youngest of four siblings, was left to run the family farm when the Depression hit. Grandpa Russell's dad, my great grandfather, George, had to travel to a Saginaw auto company for better work. The other siblings were able to attend and graduate from college, but the Depression limited the family's ability to send my Grandpa Mutch.

Dad moved with Grandpa and Grandma Mutch to nearby West Branch, Michigan, when Dad was three years old. Good jobs were hard to secure, but Grandpa eventually got a job as a rural mail carrier. They eventually built a house on Fremont Street with a perfect little brook trout stream running through the backyard. Years later, on trips to Grandma's house, brother Dave and I couldn't wait to get out of the car to fish that little secret spot just upstream from the footbridge. Grandpa and Dad spent countless hours fishing and hunting together. Many of his hunting trips were spent at their family deer camp just up the road in Saint Helen.

In high school, Dad found time for sports, excelling in football and tennis. He was an all-conference football halfback and even attempted to play for Ferris State College. His tennis talents took him on a path toward state competition in pairs. Interestingly, it was his tennis coach and the coach's wife that set Dad up on the blind date to meet Mom. As fate would have it, the tennis coach's wife was Mom's sister, Peggy.

Dad had decided to go to Michigan State College of Agriculture and Applied Science and major in forestry. When he changed his mind and decided to pursue pharmacy at Ferris, the college had already filled up with returning war vets on the GI Bill. So, he stayed in Lansing his freshman year, waiting to get into the pharmacy program at Ferris. The next year, they both transferred to Ferris. One year later, Dad sold his riding horse that he always kept boarded on a small farm outside of West Branch to buy Mom's engagement ring.

Mom and Dad were married in Gaylord on August 31, 1950, on Dad's birthday. One year later, they finally had time for a honeymoon—paddling and camping on the Au Sable River. Together they finished their degrees at Ferris. Dad completed pharmacy school and Mom got her teaching degree. Mom and Dad moved to West Branch for several years and finally to Marlette to work for my Dad's aunt and uncle, both pharmacists, at their store, Robinsons Rexall Drug Store.

Our family grew with the addition of Dave, Becky, Sam, and me. I was a young boy when Grandpa and Grandma Dudd retired as caretakers of the Vanderbilt Club and moved into Vanderbilt in the late 1950s. They retired shortly after the Club owners decided to sell the property to Alan Gornick. John and Ann Miller, parents of Mom's classmate, Ruth, took over as caretakers. At the time, Mr. Gornick was Tax Counsel and Director, Office of Tax Affairs for Ford Motor Company. I spoke with his son, Keith Gornick, about his Club memories. He remembers the Club fondly and describes the Club as a beautiful piece of river property.

This 2006 Leadership Legends honor given by the Gaylord Chamber of Commerce to Alan Gornick is on display at the Otsego Historical Museum:

> *"He came to Detroit in 1946 as a tax counsel for the Ford family and the Ford Motor Company, eventually creating a structure for Ford's initial public stock offering in 1956 through which the Ford family has been able to maintain voting control of the company to this day. He bought the Otsego Club in 1955 (from the estate of Don McLouth) and immediately built – The Classic – golf course, thus turning his labor of love into a year-round destination. When the local school system could not afford an auditorium in its new high school, Gornick and his family donated land for sale that led to funding the construction of the Alan L. Gornick Auditorium, a first class performing arts center for the Gaylord area and Northern Michigan."*

Ford Motor Company

ALAN L. GORNICK
TAX COUNSEL AND
DIRECTOR, OFFICE OF TAX AFFAIRS

3000 SCHAEFER ROAD
DEARBORN, MICHIGAN

September 18, 1956

Mrs. Vernon E. Dudd
Vanderbilt Club
Vanderbilt, Michigan

Dear Mrs. Dudd:

    I am enclosing herewith my check in the amount of $52.00 covering the Vanderbilt Club invoice for the period September 1 to 3.

    With kindest regards, I remain

Sincerely,

Alan Gornick

Encl. (1)

The last two letters in Grandma's collections of saved letters from Club members marked the end of their 27 years as Caretakers at the Vanderbilt Club.

DRURY L. PORTER
LANSING, MICHIGAN

10-8-56

Dear Dudd's:

Am enclosing this check for your last service charge, it is pretty hard to do this after 28 years at our Vanderbilt Club and I say our's because you have been as much if not more of the Club than the 3 remaining. I have very deep regrets when I realize that we have come to the parting of our paths.

For Mrs. Porter and myself may I say that we three years past enjoyed every minute spent at the Club which has been made possible by the fine cooperation and effort to please by all the Dudd's.

I am sorry to advise that Mr. Gornick's attorney informs me that he will not return from California until Oct. 25 and has requested we extend final payment on the sale to Oct. 29th, which I have agreed to do.

I mention this so you will undstand that I cannot do anything about the Holden account until the sale has been completed

The Porter's hope if you come to Lansing during the Holidays that we may have the pleasure of seeing you.

Cordialy yours

Drury L. Porter

Grandma Dudd and me at the Club, 1954

Even though I was quite young when Grandma and Grandpa finally retired, I do remember eating in the Club kitchen and taking scraps of bread to the back porch where we hand-fed the raccoons.

> *"It's sad, for me, to look upon the Club as it stands now with dry eyes. Mom's memories are many and vivid. Mine are few and somewhat cloudy, but I do remember the buildings. In particular, I can recall evenings we would sit around the kitchen table after the dishes were done and talk. The 9:00 PM announcement by the whip-poor-will was a soothing reminder that another day was done and dark was upon us. Soon after, Grandma would give us kids a few scraps of bread and we would open the screen door in anticipation of greeting the regular nightly guests. Quite often they would be lying, outstretched, along the logs that covered the back porch. From our tiny hands to theirs, we would feed these masked visitors until the scraps were gone. Standing in the burned out ruin that now remains, I can still see Grandma, Grandpa, Mom and Dad all talking around the ghost** of the kitchen table."*
>
> *Pete Mutch memo, written late 1990s*

**Ghost of the kitchen table—for several years we collected Charles Petterson prints. Many of his prints captured the current condition of a location or event with a background, ghost-like image, of it's past glory.

Grandma, brother Dave, and me (left) feeding the nightly guests

Me at the steps of the Club house holding one of my first fish (the river and engine house in the background)

Me in front of the old engine house

Chapter 4

One by one, the big clubs began to disappear, signaling the end of an era. Properties were being subdivided, sold to individuals or other private groups. The state of Michigan aggressively pursued much of this land and still does.

Initially, in April 1919, the state designated 6,468 acres east of Vanderbilt as the Pigeon River State Forest. Most of this land was abandoned by the large lumber companies and some individuals because they failed to pay their taxes. Much of this land was cutover forests and no longer profitable. Many others failed at their attempt to farm these poor soils. Nearby state lands, purchased largely with hunting license fees, were gradually merged into the forest system.

Beginning in the 1970s, the state, with its new infusion of cash from oil royalties, has added more acreage to the Pigeon River Country. This money is placed into The Natural Resource Trust Fund, established to purchase land for public use, and the fund is now valued at over one billion dollars. Very large pieces of private land were bought with monies generated from oil royalties and other funds: Green Timbers, 6,440 acres; Blue Lakes Ranch, 2,608 acres; and Mud Lake, Walled Lake, Story Lake, and most recently, 597 acres of Black River Ranch property. Today, the Pigeon River forest boundary now contains well over one hundred thousand acres with less than 10 percent in private hands.

My North News Service on July 15, 2019, describes the Pigeon River Forest, "at 107,600 acres, Pigeon River Country is the largest block of continuous undeveloped land in Michigan's Lower Peninsula. (It's half the size of New York City—12 miles wide and 20 miles long.)"

On many occasions, we would travel "out east"; this is what Mom called the Pigeon once Grandma and Grandpa moved into town. Many of those years were spent on the property owned by Dr. Sibley Hoobler—a professor at the University of Michigan Medical School. His dad, Dr. B. Raymond Hoobler, and then Sibley, owned a large piece of river property across the road from the Club and knew Mom, Grandma, and Grandpa during their caretaking years.

Grandpa would occasionally need to bring Sibley to the Club to answer a phone call (apparently the club had a phone before the Hooblers installed one). Even after Grandpa and Grandma moved into town, Sibley would stop by their house on his way out to his camp to borrow a can of coffee. He would tell us to contact his caretaker to open the back gate, and we could drive to a campsite he let us use. Mom always insisted that we didn't go near the Hooblers' cabins so as not to bother him or his guests.

```
                B. RAYMOND HOOBLER, M. D.
                     808 THREE MILE DRIVE
                   GROSSE POINTE PARK, MICH.

                              February 15, 1943


    My dear Vern:

    Thank you so much for stopping in at the cabin and
    reporting on the open front door. I am sending
    you under separate cover a bunch of keys from which
    you will find the key to the back door. The front
    door is supposed to be locked with a spike put through
    the latch to hold it shut. Apparently the wind was
    so strong that it tore the latch loose. I would
    appreciate it greatly if you would go into the cabin
    and see that the door is shut securely, even if you
    have to nail the spike into the log to make sure that
    it holds the door shut.

    I enjoyed your description of the winter and am glad
    you are housed in Vanderbilt and not at the Club.

    Hoping to see you soon and thanking you, I am

                          Cordially yours,

                          BR Hoobler
                          B. Raymond Hoobler

    BRH:M
```

Dr. Raymond Hoobler letter (Sibley's dad)

The Hoobler back gate

Dave, Becky, Sam, and I have many wonderful memories of our days spent with Mom and Dad up north on the Pigeon River. Dad taught all of us how to river fish on the Hoobler property. We were barely big enough to keep waders on or even stand up in what then seemed to be deep and fast water. We would get so excited to catch anything, even if it was a brook trout smaller than the stretched-out night crawler we were using!

Eventually, Dad introduced us to fly fishing. You could fill an entire fly box with the flies we left on the tag alders along that stretch of the Pigeon! The bridge area always seemed deeper, darker, and a little scary to wade in back then. It's not so deep and scary now that our legs have stretched out a bit. Dave caught one of his biggest trout under that bridge!

On another occasion, Dave and I fished downstream to Hoobler's cabin, played a little tennis, and then fished back upstream to our campsite.

Becky remembers speaking with Sibley after they slowly approached each other while fishing the Pigeon. As he got closer to her and the smoke from his cigar began to clear, he asked, "Did you fall in the river?" and suggested that her face was beginning to rust from all of her time in the river. Sibley was jokingly trying to explain a noble reason for all of Becky's freckles.

She also recalls Dave and me fishing in front of her and eventually disappearing out of sight. The two of us would get out of the water and sneak through woods back to where she was fishing. When she least expected it, we would scare her with wild animal sounds or create loud splashes in the water in front of her. After a while, she just expected it. The real Bigfoot could have been in the woods and I'm sure she would have just ignored it.

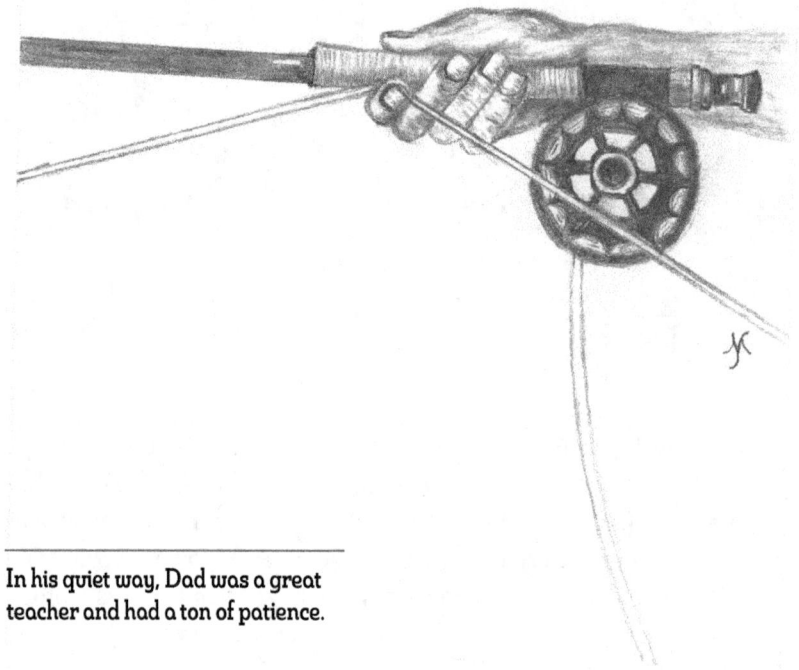

In his quiet way, Dad was a great teacher and had a ton of patience.

A potentially scary moment happened when we discovered Sam was allergic to bees while camping at Town Corners. Dad, Dave, and I took the car and ventured out to fly fish. That left Mom, Becky, and little brother, Sam, to hold down the campsite. At some point, Sam noticed a large "fuzzy-looking bee" and "decided to pet it."

Soon after his crying had quieted down, Becky tried to distract him by putting him in the front seat of the yellow canoe and venturing out onto Town Corners Lake. When Sam finally turned around to look at Becky, she was mortified—"He had no nose." They quickly went ashore and Mom proceeded to use the various medications Dad always packed for our bumps, bruises, and emergencies.

When we fishermen finally returned to the campsite, Mom and Becky looked a bit exhausted and perturbed that we left them without a car that could have allowed them to make the necessary trip to the ER in Gaylord. We couldn't see what all the fuss was about. By then, Sam looked fine to us, but we got the message.

Some of our fishing excursions with Dad took us to the Lansing Club Pond. We would drag our yellow canoe through the swamp to the "stake" in the Pigeon River located on a very small piece of state land that separated the Lansing Club from the Vanderbilt Club water. I remember the very dark water in the pond and the very soft riverbed. A few, long ago abandoned river boats were sunk with only the bows sticking out of the dark water at the river's edge. We usually caught some nice brookies for all our effort. When we were older, we would climb the fire tower and look out over the forest.

I remember the one and only time I fell in the river and totally filled my waders. It was a snow-covered opening day of trout season at Hoobler's, fishing with Dad. I can tell you it was a long, cold walk to the car parked at the back gate.

Another great fishing memory was a solo road trip from Alma College to Vanderbilt. It rained the entire weekend, but to my amazement, those two days were the best brook trout fishing at Hoobler's I've ever experienced.

Dave and me fishing at Hoobler's

Becky at Hoobler's

Dave and me at the stake between the Vanderbilt Club and the Lansing Club

Dad at the stake

Dad with little brother, Sam

Old fire tower

Vanderbilt wasn't just a summertime destination. We spent many winter weekends at Grandma and Grandpa's. Dad got every other Sunday off. On those weekends, we would leave town right after his work on Saturday night and get to Vanderbilt four hours later. Then on Sunday, we would ski at Sylvan Knob, now Tree Tops, then owned by the Meads. We had a season pass to ski at this family-friendly hill where we enjoyed our packed lunch, rope tows, and Poma lifts. We headed straight home when the hill closed.

Vanderbilt always got lots of snow. I remember sliding on Grandpa's snow shovels down the steep road in front of the Vanderbilt school and building snow caves in the big banks of snow left by the snowplow. We returned home one weekend to very snowy conditions in Marlette. Mom was shocked when Sam, at an age of no more than five, and after spending some unsupervised time with Grandpa, blurted out, "There goes the goddamn snowplow."

Vanderbilt has also been known to get pretty cold. The coldest day in Michigan history was recorded on February 9, 1934, in Vanderbilt—a chilly -51 degrees Fahrenheit.

Chapter 5

One of my biggest blessings is to have shared almost my entire life with one very special person—Nan. This memoir would not be possible without her support. Nan and I went to Marlette High School together our junior and senior year. My mom actually met Nan first! Mom was substitute teaching in a typing class and Nan was one of her students. I remember my mom coming home one day after school and asking me if I knew Nancy Walkowski and suggested that if I didn't … I should!

Nan grew up in Hemans, just nine miles north of Marlette. Her entire town consisted of a general store and grain elevator. She attended the one-room country Parker School south of Hemans, just as her Dad did years before. Eventually, her school merged into the Marlette school district, and Nan and her five classmates began their sophomore year at Marlette.

Marlette had a small population of just over 1,700 and was a small class B high school at the time. The town was not big or even average size by most people's standards, but compared to other small towns in the thumb of Michigan, it was a decent size. We had several hardware stores, a couple of grocery stores, two dime stores, several clothing stores, one jeweler, a hospital, trailer factories, lots of small farms, and two pharmacies. Marlette, at the time, boasted that it had the one and only stoplight in all of Sanilac County. Our school had some great teachers. Friday nights were straight out of the movie *Hoosiers*. Day-to-day was like living in Mayberry.

Maybe it was the homecoming dance our senior year, but soon after that … the homecoming king (me) and queen (Nan) started dating. Years later, Nan's mom told me that Nan's dad, Joe, was initially concerned about Nan dating a "big city boy from Marlette." I also learned that my longer hair occasionally bothered the ex-marine, whose haircut always looked like he was still enlisted.

Soon after Nan was introduced to the family, she began working for Mom and Dad at the family drugstore after school, on holiday breaks, and summers between college, until she got her first full-time teaching job for the Bangor School District in Bay City.

Nan was included on many of our family trips to the Pigeon River and to Grandma and Grandpa Dudd's. One particularly funny story I remember was the time Nan and Sam went into hysterics as they watched Dad and me slowly disappear into the muck carrying our family yellow canoe to the stake in the Pigeon River upstream from the Lansing Club Pond. Nan said the appearance and progress resembled that of the giant (yellow) banana slugs we saw years later in the coastal forests of British Columbia.

Old yellow canoe

On another occasion while fishing at Hoobler's, our plan was for Nan to fish downstream and I would meet her there in several hours. Problem was, she never showed up! I was very relieved when I finally found her, right where I left her, sound asleep beside the river with her waders rolled up into a pillow.

I would soon realize she was the real keeper, a real trophy, and the catch of a lifetime for me. We were married on August 3, 1974, in Marlette at the Saint Michael Catholic Church, officiated by Nan's priest and my Methodist pastor—they were good golfing buddies. Our reception was at the Lamotte township hall, the meal provided by the ladies auxiliary, and our cake was made by Nan's 4-H cake decorating instructor. Erma and the Country Gentlemen provided the music entertainment. We honeymooned on Isle Royale, backpacking and fishing. We also fished the Two Hearted River in the Upper Peninsula with the waders and fly rod Dad and Mom gave Nan for her wedding gift.

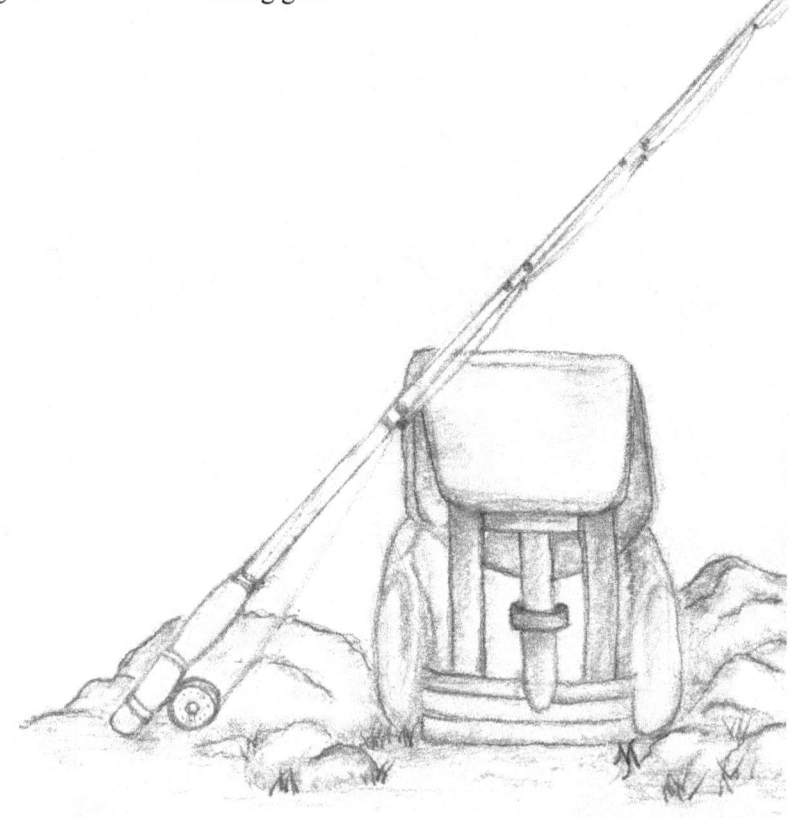

Honeymoon backpack

We went straight to married housing at Michigan State University after we returned from our honeymoon. Nan gave up her teaching job in Bay City and began substitute teaching in Holt and Mason. I had enrolled in a master's program of inter biological sciences.

One year later, I finished my master's degree and we were headed to married housing on the campus of the University of Michigan, where I was accepted into their dental school. I was dead set on going to dental school when I began my predental prerequisites at Alma College.

In fact, at one time I was even dual enrolled at Central Michigan University and Alma College to speed the process along. I was quite familiar with the CMU campus. Nan had decided to go there to pursue her teaching degree. It was less than an hour between campuses. I took my organic chemistry requirement there during my sophomore year since I couldn't get this required class until my junior year at Alma.

Along the way, my interest in science grew. In fact, I took every biology class I could and avoided, as best I could, everything else. Looking back, I can't believe the Biology Department approved my honors research proposal. I spent the winter of my senior year living at the Vestaburg Bog in a pole barn that I crudely winterized from scraps of material left over from a building project on campus. I came back to campus on the weekends to use the chemistry labs, to wash up, and to get a good meal. When I got back to my dorm room, my roommate (brother Dave) couldn't decide who smelled worse—me or McKeaver, my black Labrador retriever. You probably would not describe me as the typical well-rounded liberal arts student that Alma likes to produce.

I also had some great professors and two stood out. Every year I still get a Christmas card from Dr. Paul Roling, my Central Michigan University organic chemistry professor. He and his wife would even have Nan and me over for dinner. At Alma, my biology mentor and favorite professor was Jerry Smith. I was very saddened when the Biology Department at Alma called me over my freshman summer break and wanted me to know that he passed away, unexpectedly, from a brain aneurysm. Because of his influence and others, I started to consider additional career choices.

My master's degree allowed me to pursue even more areas of science but the end result was a rededication to dentistry. Soon after we arrived in Ann Arbor for dental school, Nan began teaching special education for the Washtenaw Intermediate School District. We were pretty much living on nickels and dimes—the only time we left campus was to go home or north to Vanderbilt. Grandma and Grandpa Dudd were always glad to see us, especially if we brought Grandpa's favorite—KFC. It was always fun listening to Grandma and Nan share their teaching stories and ideas. Grandpa Dudd passed away on August 25, 1978, at the age of eighty-four. Grandma Dudd passed away a year later on October 5, 1979, at the age of eighty.

After graduation from dental school in 1979, we moved to Lapeer, Michigan, just thirty miles from Marlette. My childhood dentist in Marlette had decided to relocate to Lapeer and he asked me to join him. At the time, I thought this would be temporary. I was also thinking of setting up a practice in Gaylord. Forty-two years later, I still love dentistry, but I'm still practicing in Lapeer.

Shortly after we arrived in Lapeer, our family started to grow. We were blessed with two great sons, Andy and Nate. After the boys finished college, they returned to the area, bringing with them their future wives. Andy married Beth Stygstra from Holland, Michigan in 2006. They have two daughters, Natalie and Elise. Nate married Kate Fager from Otsego, Michigan in 2010 and they have one daughter, Averie.

All four of us – Pete, Nan, Nate, Andy. We opened the farm in 2002.

Nan removing tree tags

Nan spent these years being the best mom and teacher. She retired from teaching special education for the Lapeer County Intermediate School District in 2019 and now totally enjoys being grandma to the little girls we never had.

We both spend much of our spare time operating Mutch's Hidden Pines Christmas Tree Farm. The entire family pitches in to help.

Our sons' sense of adventure and love of the outdoors began when they were very young.

> "We all hunt, fish, camp and enjoy the great outdoors for many different reasons. Some want to conquer these activities while others wish to become part of them. The biggest rack or largest lunker may be the ultimate goal of some, and that's fine. I tend to take a little different route pursuing my Boone and Crocket award. Much to my wife's amazement, I began taking my two boys to help open deer camp at the ages of two and three. I remember not only packing the usual gear and grub, but also taking along a sufficient supply of clean clothes (much to my wife's dismay – the boys usually returned home wearing the same clothes they wore when they left the house). ... Five years have passed and the boys wouldn't miss this yearly event for the world. They talk about it all year long. They talk of the stories Grandpa tells in front of the roaring fire, if they can keep him awake long enough; they talk about the serious card games we played—fish and crazy eights; they learn about a special great grandfather they never got to meet; and they talk of how Grandpa is always up first to make a big breakfast and how he comes into the bunk room banging on a fry pan saying 'wake up, it's morning in the swamp—time for breakfast.' One by one the boys and their two little cousins would roll out of their sleeping bags, walk across the cement floor of the tin roofed deer shack, and make their way to the breakfast table. Nathan is usually up first—he's usually the hungriest. Grandpa gave him the job of rolling the sausage links in the fry pan on the old wood cook stove. Andy's job has been to keep the two wood stoves going. He usually succeeds in doing such a fine job that we ultimately have to open a cabin door to cool the place down. Our days are spent splitting wood, walking to our

deer blinds, looking for scrapes and rubs, and eating a pack lunch in the woods while drying cold feet and wet mittens over a small fire the boys would build. Five seasons have passed since the boys started going to camp. Five seasons have passed since I last shot a deer. There has been no Boone and Crocket award lately—or has there. You see, Andy and Nathan are my awards. I'm always an award winner; a trophy getter. These trophy memories will last a lifetime. Everyone has a Boone and Crocket season even if you just take home memories."

Pete Mutch short story, written late 1980s

Drying mittens over the fire

"The Shack"

There is a place used once a year,
Out in the woods, no towns are near.

Outhouse, bunks, cobwebs galore,
Worn out furniture, no lock on the door.

Antlers, fireplace, no water at all.
Not even a phone to make a call.

This place is special to me and my dad,
His dad brought him when he was a lad.

Each November hunters gather here,
To exchange stories and hunt for deer.

I look forward to seeing this little shack
Friends and family it does not lack.

It's often filled with laughter and fun,
Once a year, until hunting season is done.

Often times we don't even get a deer.
But no matter what we come back each year.

Andy wrote this poem in 1993 at the age of thirteen for a school project and gave it to Grandpa Phil as a Christmas gift.

Andy and Nate with cousins Jeff and Sarah at our family deer camp in Saint Helen, Michigan. Brother Dave instructing and Dad supervising.

Drying mittens

Andy, Nate, and me at deer camp

As a family, we enjoyed many great outdoor adventures together—traveling the country in our pop-up camper. But, not surprisingly, we always return to the Pigeon … my home water.

Here, our family has made many great memories together—camping at the Tubes, hiking around Headquarters, blueberry picking by the sinkholes, fishing at Cornwall Floodings, looking for elk from the car and on horseback, hiking into Hoobler's, and fishing the Pigeon. On clear nights at the Pigeon River State Forest Campground (we call the "Tubes"), we would all lay on the picnic tables and watch the shooting stars. During the day, we floated down the river with inner tubes, and at night, we removed all the many bloodsuckers that had come "home" with us. I even took a pretty good spill on my bike riding on a trail close to Headquarters with Nate.

We were always busy on our trips to the Pigeon, even if some would view our occasional moments of inactivity as doing nothing. Other senses would take over: the visual explosion of fall colors and spring flowers; the welcoming smell of the river that hits you even before you can see the water; the "symphony in silence" when you take the time to just sit and listen; the taste of a handful of blueberries; and the sensation of walking on air when you cross over large carpets of thick club moss. It would take much more than a lifetime to take it all in.

Pigeon River State Forest Campground that we call the "Tubes"

Andy and I reconnected with Hoobler one year to see if we could still fish his property. The wording on his sign at the back gate had changed. A quick phone call not only reassured me that fishing was OK, but this time he wanted Andy and me to come through the front gate to his cabin so we could talk. After a nice conversation, he invited my family to use the "river cabin" whenever we wanted. The following winter I got a phone call from Sibley's daughter, Pat, saying he had passed away. She wanted me to know that he had told her about his invitation to use the cabin, and that it was still fine with their family if I chose to stay there.

	216-561-5566	Jan 2/
SIBLEY W. HOOBLER, M.D.	13515 SHAKER BLVD.	CLEVELAND, OHIO 44120

Dear Friends: I'm delighted that you've joined the P River summer club. I enclose some orientation material & hope you can share time while we're there. You need to reserve through the Haldanes — one cabin per family (or twice the rental). Everything to cook except the food is there!

There has been some reorganization: my son will acquire the south half of the section & is looking for a purchaser (at about $800/acre). Do you know of any one?

We'll be away for two months, but you can talk with my son-in-law Harold Schocker (of Meridian City) until we return.

All best —
"Doc" Hoobler

Dear friend's letter from Sibley Hoobler

Dear Pigeon River Summer Club Members & Prospects: Jan 4, 1994

This letter is to advise you concerning a reorganization but no change in your enjoyment of Camp o' Pines. Harold Schock Jr with his location in Michigan will be the new manager, instead of Raymond Hoobler. As the original donor it will always be an interest of the Sibley Hooblers to see the summer cub succeed. But we need encouragement as the summer tax bills are due so that we will encourage prompt payment of the annual dues, by reducing the amount to $135 if you send a check to Harold Schock before Jan 20. After that the des will remain at $150; if you do not come up in 1994, the dues payment will carry over one year. There will be less of a problem as most of the time both the river cabin or the guest cabin will be open for occupancy at an additional $150 per week (or two weekends) paid in advance to Harold Schock Jr, address below. The North Lodge will be available at $100 and a succeeding week will be at $150 for the cabins and $50 for the NOrth Lodge. The reservations are on a priority basis by calling the Holborns at ▮▮▮▮▮▮▮▮▮▮, but please notify them one week or more in advance if your plans change, so that others may be accomodated.   Kay & I will be at Doc's Cabin from approximately May 15 to July first, and possibly thereafter. We hope all of you, whether old-timers or new guests, will enjoy the peace and solitude of Camp o' Pines.

    Kay & Sibley Hoobler.

Please send your checks, made out to Harold Schock Jr, address: A 231 EngineeringBldg, Mich State Univ, E Lansiing, Mich. 48824. Phone ▮▮▮▮▮▮▮▮▮▮

Pigeon River summer club member letter

Obituary text:

Dr. Sibley Worth Hoobler, a retired cardiologist who founded one of the country's first hypertension clinics, died on Tuesday in Tucson, Ariz. He was 82 and lived in Cleveland.

His family said he had been wintering in Arizona as usual and died of a heart attack while playing tennis.

Dr. Hoobler directed the hypertension unit at the University of Michigan Hospital in Ann Arbor from 1947 to 1974. Under his guidance, the unit became an internationally renowned research center on high blood pressure.

He taught at the university's medical school from 1959 until 1976, when he retired. Then, for about 10 more years, he was associated with Case Western Reserve University in Cleveland as a clinical professor of medicine.

A native of Manhattan, Dr. Hoobler was a 1933 graduate of Princeton University. He earned a doctorate in science and his M.D. degree at Johns Hopkins University.

He wrote many papers and a textbook on hypertension and published a memoir, "Adventures in Medicine," in 1991. He also sponsored medical scholarships through Johns Hopkins and the University of Michigan.

An avid outdoorsman and trout fisherman, he was active in the Nature Conservancy, to which he gave 640 acres of forest in northern Michigan.

Hoobler's obituary. Courtesy of the *New York Times*.

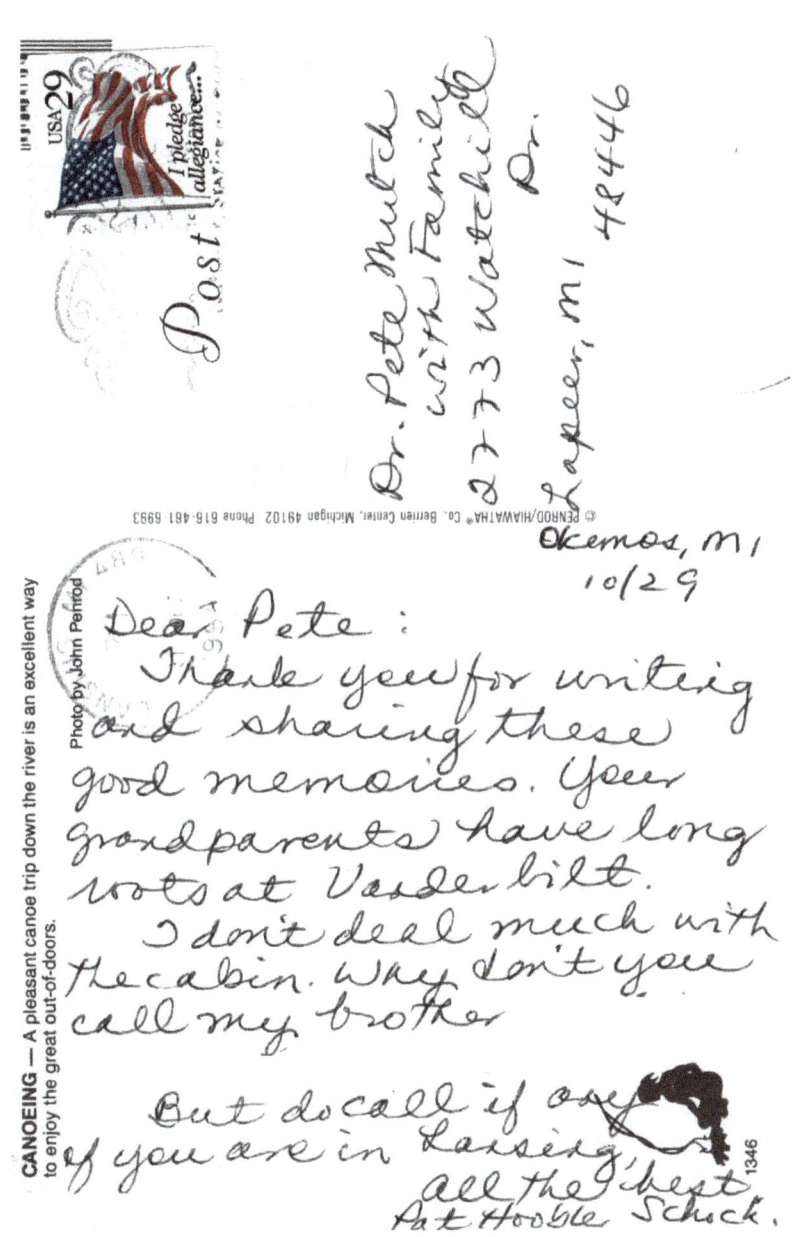

Okemos, MI
10/29

Dear Pete:

Thank you for writing and sharing these good memories. Your grandparents have long roots at Vanderbilt.

I don't deal much with the cabin. Why don't you call my brother

But do call if any of you are in Lansing.

all the best
Pat Hoobler Schock

Short letter from Pat (Hoobler) Schock

Patricia Schock

2170 Long Leaf Trail   Okemos, MI 48864

Father's Day
1994

Dear Dr. Mutch,

    Thank you for the thoughtful and kind note on Dad's passing away. I'm sure the memories are strong and special.

    I hope the summer vacation is pleasant.

                      Best wishes,
                        Pat (Hoobler)
                        Schock

Note from Pat Schock

We contacted Sibley's son, Ray Hoobler, the current owner, and on several occasions did use the cabin, taking siblings, kids, Mom, and Dad. We actually celebrated our twenty-fifth wedding anniversary at Hoobler's. Nan and I took Mom and Dad to share in our special day and to surprise my mother. She was very shocked when I drove through the front gate—not the usual back gate!

```
May 21, 1996


Dear Pete and Nan,

Thank you very much for the article on the Vanderbilt Club fire. It
sure brought back old memories! We appreciated the chance to meet
you last year, and I was delighted to have you at Camp O'Pines when
we weren't there and, also, when we were there.

It's been a long winter for us as we've had some complicated family
matters to deal with. Unfortunately we're not going to be at Camp
O'Pines for the whole summer as we had originally planned. Right
now we expect to be there for the next three weeks or so, and while
we hope to return later this summer we're not sure we'll be able
to.

We would be delighted to have you use Camp O'Pines under the same
arrangement as last year. Just let Mary and David Shaffer,
▓▓▓▓▓▓▓, know when you want to come and they'll open up the Guest
Cabin for you and your family. In return I ask for an appropriate
contribution to help keep the place operating.

But knowing that you and your family love and enjoy the Pigeon
River Country the way I do is more important than any contribution.
Sharing the place with others is part of the spirit of Camp
O'Pines, and so we are delighted to have you, your family, and
mother use the place. We look forward to seeing you again.

Yours,

Ray
```

Letter from Ray Hoobler, 1996

July 11, 1997

Dear Pete and Nan,

    This is just a brief note to bring you up to date on the cabin. As you know David and Mary quit in the middle of the winter, and so I couldn't make arrangements for anyone to see that the place was prepared for guests until we got there this spring.

After we talked on the phone I located another couple that, hopefully, will work out better. They are John and Vivian Kassuba ▮▮▮▮▮▮▮▮▮ and live in Vanderbilt. So if you are at Camp O'Pines and run into a problem, they are the ones to call.

As part of the restructuring of the family partnership that owns the property, Harold is going to keep track of guests for this year. I told him that you had called about coming up for a weekend or two. His phone is ▮▮▮▮▮▮▮▮▮, and you should call him to check on the schedule. If you do come, please make a donation as before to help cover the costs of maintaining Camp O'Pines.

I hope I've have been able to make arrangements so that your stay will be enjoyable and useful for your project. You might find someone at the Otsego County Historical Society that could help you. They have a storefront museum on Main Street in Gaylord. Please let me see a copy of anything you put together. I think it's a great idea

We will return August 3rd and stay until August 25th when Aurora and a friend are coming for a visit. It would be great to see any or all or a subset of you and your family!

Yours,

Ray Hoobler

Ray

Letter from Ray Hoobler, 1997

February 11, 2015

Dr. Peter M. Mutch and Family
303 West Newark Rd.
Lapeer, MI 48446

Dear Pete,

On behalf of the Pigeon River Country Association and our partners, I would like to thank you for your very generous contributions of $500 for the development of the Pigeon River Country Historical Interpretation Center and the promise of additional donations from others in your family. As you well know the Pigeon River Country is a special place with both a rich history and a diverse range of activities. Your support and that of others like you is crucial as we develop a Historical Interpretive Center that will educate us, our children and grandchildren about the Pigeon River Country. Your idea of contacting your mother has been passed on to the Steering Committee who were quite excited about the idea of getting oral histories. With support and some luck we hope to start construction work this summer.

This letter also certifies that you have received no goods or services in return for your contribution other than knowing that you have helped carry out our stated aim of educating visitors about the history and wild characteristics of the Pigeon River Country. Our website, www.pigeonriver.org, contains further information about this Center as well as a link to its web page on the Otsego County Historical Society website. Here you will find up to date information about current plans as well as historical material such as maps and photographs from the early 1900's.

Sincerely yours,

Raymond T. Hoobler

Raymond T. Hoobler
President, Pigeon River Country Association

Thanks, Pete. You are always welcome to stay in the man cabin. Your family support is great. We are just in initial planning stages now. Stay in touch!

Letter from Ray Hoobler, 2015

My family owes a great deal of gratitude to the Hoobler family. We camped throughout the forest, but we always made time to venture into Hoobler's. At the time, it felt like the Pigeon River Forest and Hoobler's were one in the same. I feel this special connection kept our family coming back and provided all of us with conversation and thought throughout the year. If a Hoobler family member ever has the occasion to read my book, I extend to you and your family a heartfelt "Thank you!" I was shocked and saddened to hear the news that Ray Hoobler passed away from COVID in April 2020. So sad ... I also wished he could have read my book.

Ray Hoobler remembered as Pigeon forest advocate

Special to the Herald Times
The Petoskey News-Review

OTSEGO COUNTY — Raymond Hoobler, longtime advocate for protecting and supporting the Pigeon River Country east of Vanderbilt, has died of COVID-19 in New York City's Mount Sinai Hospital.

Hoobler, 78, a retired professor of mathematics at City University New York (CUNY), spent summers at the family property, Camp o'Pines, on the Pigeon River, where he was the third generation of advocates for the wild character of the nearby Pigeon River Country State Forest. He had been a board member of the Pigeon River Country Association since 1995 and president of that organization for 17 of those years from 1998 to 2015, and was currently the association secretary.

His father, Sibley Hoobler, was one of the original members of the association, which organized in 1972 to protect the forest from the oil and gas exploitation that was underway through permits issued by the state of Michigan. The association's efforts led to the state forest being officially established as Pigeon River Country, with hydrocarbon development restricted to the southern third of the forest, and the formation of the state forest system's only citizens advisory council under a formal Concept of Management.

Ray's grandfather, Bert Raymond Hoobler, was a pediatrician who grew up on the Pigeon property and was an early advocate of setting aside the nearby forest lands for public use. Bert's son Sibley, Ray's father, became a physician known for pioneering work in hypertension. He died in 1994, shortly before Ray became active in Pigeon River Country Association efforts to protect the forest.

....

Ray and his wife, Frances Kuehn, lived in New York City and spent mid-May to mid-September at Camp o'Pines. Frances, a noted artist, and Ray were married at Camp o'Pines in 1990....

....

Hoobler was a professor emeritus at City College and the Graduate Center, which are among 25 campuses of CUNY across five boroughs. CUNY is a public university, serving a large percentage of first-generation-educated students. He continued counseling math students after retirement. He also established funding for Vanderbilt, Michigan, students going beyond high school, through the Otsego Community Foundation.

....

Hoobler's own undergraduate degree was from Oberlin College in Ohio, his Ph.D. from Berkeley, with some additional work at Columbia.

He was born Aug. 14, 1941, in Boston, Massachusetts. He became symptomatic with COVID-19 on April 6, 2020, entered Mount Sinai on April 16, and died on April 29.

Petoskey News-Review article, 2020

With one exception, we had no access to the Club property once Grandma and Grandpa retired in 1956, shortly after Alan Gornick bought it. I remember on this one occasion that Grandma's brother, my great uncle Andy, a bank executive in Lansing, came to visit Grandma. He decided to drive out to the Club property to see what changes had occurred since Grandma's retirement years prior.

He stopped the car in front of the old Club gate. He hopped over the gate before Nan and I were even out of the car. I yelled ahead to him, "Did you see the no trespassing signs?" The property was clearly marked.

He yelled back, "I didn't see anything." I really don't remember the rest of our adventure—I was too afraid of being caught.

Shortly after Alan Gornick's purchase of the 312-acre Club property in 1956, several other members were added. William F. Thomas, Fred A. Knorr, and Gordon J. McMullen became members on July 1, 1958. In the early 1960s, Roy Fruehauf bought Fred Knorr's 25 percent interest. Then on November 8, 1963, Gornick, McMullen, and Fruehauf purchased the adjacent 325 acres to the west with its "River Cabin" from the Dumfords of Middletown, Ohio.

Upon the deaths of Thomas in 1968 and Fruehauf in 1969, Gornick and McMullen became the sole owners of the combined properties on July 15, 1969. When the Club house burned in 1971, the McMullens continued their many trips to the property and stayed in the River Cabin.

Gordon McMullen Jr. (Gordy) told me that a discussion to divide the property was started well before September 2, 1994, when the Club property was finally split. The McMullen family took the more recently added 325 acres with its River Cabin and later, in 2002, adopted the Vanderbilt Club name for estate planning purposes. Alan Gornick kept the original Vanderbilt Club acreage containing the burned-out footprint of the old lodge.

Gordy explained to me that the family's decision to take the 325 acres to the west with its existing River Cabin meant that they didn't have to build a new cabin. Their family has made many updates to their beautiful property and their cabin over the years and have always graciously invited me to stop in for a visit whenever I see their gate open.

PAGE TWO **Herald Times** Wednesday, April 21, 1971

Bradford Lake Lodge Damaged in Blaze

Vanderbilt Club Destroyed by Fire

Fire destroyed one landmark club, and damaged another during the past week.

In Wednesday morning, April 4, the 17-room Vanderbilt Club east of Vanderbilt was destroyed by an explosion of either a hot water heater or the furnace.

Spontaneous combustion of the oil furnace is believed to have caused much smoke damage and some fire damage to the Bradford Lake Lodge, west of Waters, on Tuesday, April 13.

"High Pines," home of the Vanderbilt Club, is presently owned by Gordon McMullen and Allen Gornick, both of Bloomfield Hills.

The fire there was discovered by Frank Schneider, who with his wife, have been caretakers at the club since September, 1970. While they were at breakfast at 7:30 they heard what they thought was a sonic boom and shortly after, Schneider discovered that the house was on fire. He and his wife were able to rescue only a few clothes.

Twenty-five volunteer firemen from Vanderbilt, with three pieces of fire-fighting equipment, arrived on the scene to fight the blaze. However, the building was a total loss and there has been an estimate of damage up to $50,000. The property was insured.

The Vanderbilt Club has been on its present site for about 90 years. A log building, it was originally built as a logging camp. Allen Gornick, one of the owners, is also a part owner of Otsego Ski Club, at Hidden Valley.

The Bradford Lake Lodge in Waters is owned by Artie O'Neil of Detroit. It is between 30 and 40 years old and is built of stone and large logs. Fire destroyed the south-east corner of the lodge, and there was much smoke damage. Edward Taylor of the Waters Fire Department said that the logs seemed to be burning from the inside out, and firemen had to break through a number of them.

The fire was discovered by Ruth Geltz who lives across the street from the lodge/She saw smoke and reportedly it to

the fire department. There was no one in the lodge at the time of the fire. Damage was minor.

The fire at Bradford Lake Lodge has focused attention again on the amount of work that it has taken to raise money for the fire truck and for the contribution made to the building of the new fire hall. The women of the community put on three dinner and several bake sales to raise the $982.95, which has been used for these purposes.

Vanderbilt Club destroyed by fire

| 110 | The Vanderbilt Club

RUINS OF VANDERBILT CLUB — Only a few logs of the walls of the 17-room lodge at the Vanderbilt Club remained standing after a fire destroyed the building Tuesday. Loss of the lodge, which overlooked the Sturgeon River 14 miles east of Vanderbilt, was estimated at $50,000. Photo by Shirley Bates.

NEARLY CENTURY OLD
Hunting Club Destroyed by Flames at Vanderbilt

VANDERBILT — The Vanderbilt Club, a privately-owned hunting and fishing club 14 miles east of here overlooking the Sturgeon River, was destroyed by fire Wednesday morning.

The two-story, log-constructed club building was owned by Gordon McMullen and Allen Gornick, both of Bloomfield Hills. The building was originally on a logging camp site and housed 17 rooms.

The blaze was reported out of control by the time the Vanderbilt Fire Department's three pieces of equipment and 25 firemen arrived at the scene. State police of the Gaylord Post estimated the loss at $50,000.

All but one wall and a portion of another collapsed in the fire. Logs were reportedly still burning some four hours after the fire broke out.

The fire was discovered about 7:30 a.m. by Mr. and Mrs. Frank Schneider, caretakers, who lived in a downstairs apartment in the clubhouse.

Mrs. Schneider said she awoke about 6 a.m. and started doing her housework. In the meantime she noticed their dog appeared extremely nervous and was pacing the floor.

Hunting club destroyed by flames

Small article continuing from previous page

Shortly after the Schneiders ate breakfast they heard a "big boom" which they believed to be a sonic boom.

Schneider noticed what he thought was fog coming from the sun shining on the frost-covered roof. When he got up and looked out he saw flames going up the side of a rear wall of the dwelling.

Mrs. Schneider believes the "boom" they heard was a gas furnace exploding.

Authorities are investigating this possibility because the fire is thought to have started in the area where the gas wall furnace was located.

The loss is reported to be covered by insurance.

There were no inuries.

The clubhouse was originally built by a group of Vanderbilt businessmen, including Dr. D. E. Winer, Frank Kelley, Charles Lafever, James McKibbon and Warren Bowman, at the turn of the century, it was deported here. It has been sold several times since then.

VANDERBILT CLUB -- This is all that remains of the Vanderbilt -- only a few logs of the 17-room lodge. The fire broke out Tuesday, April 13. Damage was estimated at $50,000. (Photos by Shirley Bates)

Picture of smoke and the Club

Home 7 p.m.
Wed.

Dear kids —

Fire completely destroyed the Vanderbilt Club about 8:30 a.m. today. We saw the fire equipment go east & shortly after Eulah called to tell us about it, but no particulars. When Bill came home from town he had learned that fire was caused by furnace explosion. Caretakers were eating breakfast when they heard the explosion, but thought it was a sonic bomb. Upon investigating they found the ladys room a mass of flames. Nothing was saved except a few of the caretakers clothes. Garvick happened to be at Hidden Valley, so got out to the Club in a short time. He made the statement that he could always re-build the club, but he could never replace the old pictures, clocks etc. Club is valued at $50,000. We intend to call him later on tonight & offer him any pictures that we have, to have reproductions made. I'sure

has many memories, some good, some bad, but it was our home for 27½ yrs. Snow going fast, but it remains cold - North west wind. temp. this a.m. was 18°. Jim Carter & family spent about 2 hrs with us Monday evening - on their way home, having skiied at Payne Mt. Peg called Easter Sunday - said Tom had passed his physical & would leave June 3 - (Guess I told you that already). No other news - Write
Hurriedly - Mom -

Letter from Grandma

Just after the property was divided in 1994, the Gornicks donated their Club property to the Gaylord Community Schools, stipulating that monies generated from its sale at a public auction would be used to finish the school auditorium. After a rather heated bidding war, the Pottingers, from Goshen, Indiana, outbid the state of Michigan for the title to the land.

Dave Pottinger had worked for the plastics industry in Detroit but "retired" at the age of forty-one, he claims, to return to Indiana, where he became heavily involved in real estate and city redevelopment and is largely credited with the restoration of downtown Goshen. He also maintained an art and antique business in New York. He was known nationally as a collector of antique quilts and three books were published about his collections. Hundreds of his quilts have been acquired by major U.S. museums.

I asked Dave if going up against the state at the public auction for the Club property was a bit nerve-racking. He said, "Not really, I rather enjoyed it. I've been involved with auctions and the bidding process most of my adult life. The individual bidding for the state seemed much more nervous than I was."

For years, Dave and Faye have had a cabin on the Black River, just two miles past the gate of the Vanderbilt Club. His cabin and the area still provides a much-needed respite from his pretty busy life.

October 20, 1994

DNR loses school land bid

By DAN HEATON
Assistant Editor

Permit request up next; p. A-15

GAYLORD — A 312-acre piece of land next to the Pigeon River Country State Forest will remain in private hands, despite an all-out lobbying effort by the Dept. of Natural Resources (DNR) to lay claim to it.

The Gaylord Community Schools Board of Education Monday voted 5-2 to sell the property to high bidders Dave and Fay Pottinger of Goshen, IN, for $470,000. The DNR bid $461,000 to buy the land, donated to the school last month by the Gornick family on the condition it be sold and proceeds from that sale be used to fund completion of the auditorium — to be dubbed the Alan L. Gornick Auditorium — at the new Gaylord High.

VOTING IN FAVOR of the measure were board president Chris Collins and trustees Susan Bensinger, Gerry Campbell, Marilyn Crawford and Chuck Veeser.

See DNR, p. A-15

DNR loses school land bid

INSIDE

DNR lobbying effort failure; school sells to private buyers

Cont'd from p. A-1

Trustees Jackson Riling and Edith Sims voted against the motion made by Bensinger.

Although the school awarded the sale of the land — which contains almost a mile of the Pigeon River, part of the Lansing Club pond and the site of the old Vanderbilt Club clubhouse that burned down a generation ago. That requires a special use permit from the Pigeon River Zoning Board.

IF THE POTTINGERS can't get the permit, the sale of the land would then go to the DNR.

A long list of people addressed the school board on Monday night, lobbying the school board to vote a particular way. Collins said the board had received "a large selection" of letters on the issue and had been lobbied verbally extensively in the days between Monday's vote and last Wednesday's public auction for the land.

That auction drove the selling price up $100,000 over the appraised value and starting bid point for the land of $364,000.

Dave Pottinger said that had he and his wife not bid on the land, the school board would have accepted the $364,000 original bid from the DNR. "So what you have here isn't a case of us having a bid of $9,000 more than the state, whatever you do, you will realize $100,000 more than you expected. And after this money is gone and the auditorium is built, I suspect that if I walked into the school and handed (Supt.) Mason (Buckingham) a check for $9,000, that would be a big deal."

DNR officials' appeal to the board was supported by representatives of the the Elkland Seniors Conservation Club, Pigeon River Country State Forest Advisory Council and Association, Trout Unlimited, Northland Sportsman's Club, the Ruffed Grouse Society and Kiwanis Club, as well as several private citizens and local DNR employees.

"While we were not the successful bidder, we believe we were successful in letting this community know of our interest in the property," said Rodney Stokes, head of the DNR's real estate division.

Stokes said the DNR had attempted to purchase the property from the Gornicks directly in years past.

"There is support both statewide and locally to have that land publicly owned and publicly held," Stokes said. "We believe the benefits of public ownership far outweigh the benefits of the few extra dollars the school would realize."

KEN MUDGET, president of the Elkland Seniors Conservation Club, presented a three-point argument for the land to be sold to the DNR and remain open to the public:

• Historic significance of the area from the days of the old Vanderbilt Club.

• Number of bald eagles, osprey, common loons and other animals and rock moss, purple lady slippers, arbutus and other plant life that is endangered or threatened. Mudget said if the land was publicly held it would allow the club to build nesting perches in the Lansing Club Pond to assist the osprey and loons.

• Possibility of the school "adopting" the area and using it as "an environmental classroom." That idea was also put forward by the DNR.

Although fewer people spoke on behalf of the Pottingers, those who did often drew some applause or words of support. One speaker came forward from the dozen or so high school students in attendance at the meeting, fulfilling a class assignment.

"This man (Pottinger) is not going to pick this land up and move

DNR lobbying effort failure/DNR loses school land bid

NEWS

PIGEON ZONE
Building needs zoning board approval

Shaded area shows property.

VANDERBILT — Although the Gaylord school board has awarded sale of 312 acres of land along the Pigeon River to an Indiana couple, they still need approval from another board, one that is little known and has only met once.

Dave and Fay Pottinger will be seeking approval from the Pigeon River Zoning Board — a board that has met only once, — to build a year-round log cabin home on the foundation of the Vanderbilt Club that once stood on the land, but was destroyed by fire years ago.

Since that foundation lies less than 200 feet from the river, the special zoning board must approve any building plans. The Pigeon River is one of 14 across the state designated as a scenic and natural river, requiring special protection.

Joe Jarecki, manager of the Pigeon River State Forest, joins appointees from the Pigeon River State Forest Advisory Council, the Otsego County Zoning Dept., the Otsego County Board of Commissioners, and Corwith Township on the zoning board. The only time the board met in the past was to consider a request from the Song of the Morning Ranch to build on a site where fire had destroyed a building that was within 200 feet of the river.

After the 1992 meeting, the Song of the Morning Ranch withdrew its request for a permit and the board never officially took any action.

JARECKI EXPLAINED the Natural Rivers Act allows the county zoning board to handle requests for special permits, but in Otsego County, since the issue has come up so seldom, the county has opted to have the state handle the matters.

"Given that so much of the land is state owned or held privately in such large parcels, the county knew it would seldom come up. In Cheboygan County, there are a few more of these issues and the county does handle zoning matters along the river," Jarecki said.

Jarecki said three original buildings still stand at the site of the Vanderbilt Club, and one virtually touches the river.

"The act allows the Pottingers to remodel those buildings without zoning variances being granted. It is the new construction the act seeks to control," he said.

According to the issue passed by the Board of Education Monday, if the Pottingers are unable to get the variance from the board, the sale of the land could instead go to the Dept. of Natural Resources.

it away. It will still be there," said Chris Pichans, a GHS senior. "He seems like the kind of man who respects the forest, and if he sees someone walking in the river trout fishing, he won't chase him away, but let him enjoy the forest, too."

Corwith Township Supervisor Vern Kassuba and Larry Higgins of Higgins Industries also spoke in favor of awarding the bid to the Pottingers.

"The way I have seen the DNR take care of what they have now, they don't need anymore land," Kassuba said.

Pigeon Zone permit request mentioned in DNR Loses School Land Bid article

New chapter ahead in st

Vanderbilt Club dates back to turn of century

By DAN HEATON
Assistant Editor

VANDERBILT — After it was destroyed by fire in April of 1971, few people talked much, or even thought much, about the old Vanderbilt Club, a long-defunct hunting and fishing club on a healthy slice of God's Country, aka, the Pigeon River Country State Forest.

That changed some last month when an Indiana couple and the Michigan Dept. of Natural Resources became embroiled in a short-lived bidding war over the rights to buy the property. The battle brought out sharp opinions of what should be done with the piece of land.

Patricia Mutch, who some of the older folks in the Vanderbilt area may remember better as Patty Dudd, is anxious about what will become of the land. She has high hopes the couple who ended up with title to the property, Dave and Fay Pottinger of Goshen, IN, will come to love it as she once did.

MUTCH WAS born at the Vanderbilt Club's lodge in 1929, just a month or so after her parents had signed on as the caretakers there.

The club dates back to the days before the turn of the century when a group of businessmen in the Vanderbilt area — doctors and dentists mostly — joined with a few Gaylord colleagues and bought an old lumber camp on the Pigeon River that was no longer in use.

Sometime in the 1890s, maybe the 1880s, the logging camp was built.

Once all the trees were gone, the loggers left and the local elite decided the spot would make a nice club.

In the early or mid-'20s, the Lansing Club (which now is the area where the Song of the Morning Ranch is located) was begun by some Lansing area automotive executives.

Within a few years, some of their friends and co-workers had their eyes set on making the neighboring Vanderbilt Club — just a short hike up the trout-laden Pigeon River — their very own.

In October of 1929, nine executives of the Wheel Motor Corp. in Lansing and their families bought the club and hired the Dudds on as caretakers.

"There sure are a lot of memories out there," Mutch said from her Reed City area home.

The club underwent an extensive remodeling after the Wheel Motor people took it over and Mutch and her sister had bedrooms in what later became a wood and tool shed.

Looking over the letter her mother wrote to her telling Mutch about the fire that destroyed her own home, Mutch recalls the sad feeling she had upon learning that news.

"THE THINGS that were lost. Navaho rugs and the beautiful brass clocks. There was a big poker table and I can still see the men sitting around that table, playing poker after spending the day hunting or fishing," she said.

"I could just cry when I think about how beautiful it once was and how it was left to go," she said.

Don Karslake, a lifelong resident of Vanderbilt, recalls when his father would operate a coach service from the train stop in Vanderbilt and would take the club members out to the lodge.

"They had quite a little bit of activity out there during the hunting season and I recall that several of the men who went out there were fishermen, too. They would bring up their gear with them and dad would drive them out," Karslake said.

"It was mostly hunting and fishing and just the men would

THE VANDERBILT CLUB and how it looked during a party sometime believed to be in the 1930s. The photo is a 1992 reprint of the original that is owned by the Otsego County His-

come. Occasionally they would bring their families. There was one family who would come for two weeks every year to try to escape hay fever problems," Mutch said.

In 1994, the road that one must travel to get to the site of the old club site remains dirt. It is rough in many places.

IN THE '30S and '40s, when Mutch and her sister and parents were living at the club, that road was impassable in the winter months, meaning she would board in Vanderbilt during the week so she could attend school. She would come home on the weekends.

"I couldn't start school until second grade because we couldn't get in and out, but mom was a school teacher so she was able to keep me up on my studies," Mutch explains. Mrs. Dudd later taught in the Vanderbilt Area School, retiring there.

As Mutch grew up, the family eventually started living in Vanderbilt during the winter months and her father would work at the Vanderbilt Ski Club, the precursor to the Otsego Ski Club at Hidden Valley, during the winter months when things were quiet at the club.

"The club was just part of another time. The members faded away and when the fire hit, I knew that was the end. I am so excited to see that someone else will be enjoying my old home now," Mutch said.

SUBSCRIPTIONS 517-732-1111

Herald Times Thursday NOV 3, 1994

RNVIEW

tory of old club

...torical Society. The reproduction was made by Bud Palin of Gaylord. Another shot of the same photo hangs at the Gateway Restaurant in Vanderbilt.

Sale of Vanderbilt property will boost new auditorium

GAYLORD — Gaylord school officials are still shooting for a Dec. 1 opening of the new auditorium at Gaylord High School, but the work on the building may last well into the New Year.

Supt. Mason Buckingham said the work on installing the ceiling, stage flooring and seats is taking longer than expected because other work on the project was behind schedule and the auditorium was completely enclosed earlier in the process than the construction people would have liked.

"That means they couldn't get their heavy-duty lift truck in there and so they are using a scaffolding that they have to move by hand to hang the ceiling. It is a very slow process," Buckingham said.

After contractors finish the work on the basic portion of the building, they will begin adding the "extras" that will be purchased using funds from the sale of 312 acres of land donated to the school by the Alan Gornick family.

About $200,000-$250,000 will be spent adding a sophisticated lighting and sound system in the auditorium. The funds will also pay for a curtain system and an acoustical shell that will be used during musical performances in the auditorium. Buckingham said school officials are also considering purchasing a grand piano that would be used in the auditorium.

THE SALE OF THE Gornick land brought $470,000 to the school, meaning another $200,000 or more will be left over after the auditorium, to be dubbed the Alan L. Gornick Auditorium, is completed. The leftover money will be spent on other school projects, Buckingham said.

Where the left-over dollars are spent exactly will be decided by a committee of Buckingham, Keith Gornick, Alan's son; and Bill Rolinski, attorney for the family.

"We've put together a list of things we would like to be able to add to our school system. I'll take that list to our committee meeting and the three of us can set some priorities," Buckingham said.

NEWS 732-1411

River zone an issue for property

VANDERBILT — A zoning board may not need to be convened to decide on building plans for an Indiana couple who recently bought 312 acres along the Pigeon River from the Gaylord schools.

Joe Jarecki, manager of the Pigeon River Country State Forest, said Dave and Fay Pottinger are also looking at sites on the land between 200 feet and 400 feet off of the river as a possible building site. Building in that distance range from the river requires the approval of Jan Fenske, a Dept. of Natural Resources zoning administrator who works at the DNR's regional headquarters in Roscommon.

The zoning board would need to approve a project only if it were within 200 feet of the river. The foundation of the old Vanderbilt Club, which was destroyed by fire in 1971, is within 200 feet of the river, and has been identified by the Pottingers as a likely building location.

The Pottingers bought the land from the Gaylord Community Schools last month for $470,000, outbidding the DNR by $9,000 for the land.

> **"Individual retirement annuity? Check with me for competitive rates."**

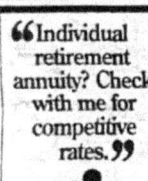

CALL ME.
Carrie C. Prendergast
621 W. Second
Gaylord, MI
517-732-4610

State Farm
Life Insurance Company
Home Office: Bloomington, Illinois

Like a good neighbor, State Farm is there.®

Gil Ziegler or Bart Stupak... The Choice Is Clear!

| BART STUPAK... | GIL ZIEGLER... |

Oct 20, '94

Editorials
School board acted appropriately in sale

Applause today for the Gaylord Community Schools Board of Education. The board did not blink when the State of Michigan was trying to stare it down.

The school board appropriately awarded a 312-acre parcel of land that borders the Pigeon River Country State Forest to a couple from Indiana, Dave and Fay Pottinger. The land had been given to the school by the Gornick family to be sold to raise funds for the school's new auditorium.

After an intense lobbying effort by the Dept. of Natural Resources (DNR), the school awarded the land to the high bidders, the Pottingers. The DNR brought forward a laundry lists of all of its public good deeds and thoughts of a possible learning laboratory for the schools that could be created on the land to enhance the education of students.

The DNR has 97,000 other acres in the Pigeon River Country State Forest. Now that this land sale went elsewhere, does the offer to make a learning lab still stand? Surely there is room somewhere else in the forest.

AS FOR the DNR's good deeds, isn't that why we pay state taxes? The agency had better have good deeds to show for them.

The Pottingers seem like decent people, but even if they weren't, who they are should have no bearing on this decision. They were living out their part of the American Dream. Through fortune, hard work or luck, they were able to buy their own slice of heaven on Earth.

If the board is having any second thoughts on that sale this morning they should remember from where the land came. Alan Gornick was a lawyer and businessman who, no doubt, followed good business practices to be able to buy the Otsego Ski Club and so much additional land in northern Michigan.

We doubt he achieved his station in life by selling to the low bidder.

Editorial: School board acted appropriately

Pottinger Family Wins PR Property Bid

by Tom Serino

A public hearing which probably should never have been necessary resulted in a Gaylord School Board decision to turn over a historical piece of the Pigeon River Forest to the Pottinger family of Indiana, for a price of $470,000

Dale and Fay Pottinger, a family in the antique business from Goshen Indiana, had submitted a final bid of $470,000 for a 312-acre piece of property, known as the Old Vanderbilt Club, totally surrounded by forest east of Vanderbilt. The only other bidder was the Michigan DNR, with their original $364,000 bid. After the Pottingers put in a $390,000 bid, the DNR continually upped the ante until the Pottingers put in a final bid of $470,000. That was last Wednesday and a special meeting was set for Monday, Oct. 17th for a decision.

After the public input, a motion was made for the sale to go to the highest bidder, with the stipulation that if the sale was not consummated within 60 days, the sale would go to the DNR. That resulted in a split vote of the School Board, 5 for and 2 against.

While OUR HOME TOWN opposes DNR takeover of private lands, OHT staff writer Ken Mudget was in favor of the sale, for the preservation of the property, and the benefit to the Gaylord Schools. Mudget proposed the Gaylord School pursue an adopt-a-forest plan, similar to that of the Vanderbilt Area Schools. Under this plan, students from Vandy adventure into the forest, into an 'adopted' area, and provide environmental clean-up and maintenance of the forest, learning about conservation of the PR.

Mudget, however, after meeting with the Pottinger family at Monday nights meeting, was satisfied that the Pottingers were environmentally conscious and wanted to keep the 312 acres in its present state, with the only change, which was to build a log-style home on the actual site of the Old Vanderbilt Clubhouse foundation. Fears of a subdivision in the forest were put away.

Pottinger family wins Pigeon River property bid

Dave Pottinger explained to me that shortly after the auction sale, he sold the northern 135 acres across the river to Skiba of Gaylord and sold about ninety acres to one of the Song of the Morning members. The end result left him with ninety acres of land, three quarters of a mile of Pigeon River frontage, and the original site of the Vanderbilt Club building.

He told me that, initially, he was going to build on the property. He loved the open view of the river from the bluff above the old lodge site. On the other hand, his wife loved the seclusion of the thick woods surrounding their current cabin a few miles down the road on the Black River. Without a healthy family consensus to build, they kept the property as is, until they finally placed it into the Headwaters Land Conservancy in 2009. This still kept the property private and in his name, but it limited any further division or development. It did allow for two future building sites.

I have been writing to Dave Pottinger for many years. He has been very generous to allow us access to the Club property. We ventured into the Club for the first time in the late 1990s. I stayed at Hoobler's one week and spent several days exploring the property with Mom, Dad, Nan, and the boys. There was still a lot of evidence from the fire that occurred almost twenty-five years before.

> "The Club, as we grew up to call it, looks much different today than what Mom describes. The club house lies as a charred ruin, the result of a fire that overtook it in April of 1971. A few blackened log walls still exist along with a brick fireplace and chimney that seems to stand just as lonely and straight as the trunks of the large white pines that now surround the place. Mother Nature has done its part in trying to envelop what remains of the building. A nice soft layer of pine needles and leaves have annually fallen and decomposed to provide a new type of floor replacing the beautifully hand rubbed yellow pine boards. The new floor now supports the little critters and dirt that Grandma and Mom tried so hard to keep out. Small descendants of the white pine nearby now grow under the ghost of the kitchen table."
>
> Pete Mutch memo, written late 1990s

Lonely chimney

Little critters and dirt Grandma tried to keep out

The Club house was a total loss

Mom's house

I fished and explored the Club on multiple occasions until that memorable fish camp week in 2009. Even though much was gone and cleaned up since the fire, Mom's memories were still vivid. She reviewed with us all the landmarks and related stories—some we had heard before and some were new. She thoroughly enjoyed talking about the Club—the good times and the bad. She pointed out where buildings had stood, the location of her birthday tree that had been planted over eighty years ago, where the old bridge existed, and where flags were raised when members visited.

The tool shed/chicken coop (previously her sleeping quarters as a child) and D.B. Lee's Place (the outhouse) were still standing. She never did say or recall why the outhouse was named for D.B. Lee. Lee was affiliated with the Lansing Club, an auto executive with the Nash Company and an early partner with George Mason to a large piece of property on the South Branch of the Au Sable River. This beautiful property, fifteen hundred acres, known as the Mason Tract, was eventually donated to the state by George Mason in 1954. I can imagine all kinds of potential reasons to name an outhouse after someone, but nothing flattering comes to mind.

Mom standing where the Vanderbilt Club lodge stood

Mom's birthday tree

Mom's house

Fireplace chimney

D.B. Lee outhouse

"Even though the physical structure no longer exists, nature has continued to evolve. Trees are much bigger—there is now shade where there was none. The path to the outhouse is over grown, making its destination difficult to locate. Oddly enough, some of Grandma's flowers planted by the entrance gate still come up every year. So, in some ways, I'm sure, Grandma still tends these flowers today."

Pete Mutch memo, written late 1990s

Roses by the front gate

In a much-treasured Club photo album that Mom and Dad had given to all of us kids, she concluded that she "can still close her eyes and see, smell, and hear the Club and the Pigeon, not the burned-out wreck it is today." Pottinger was not aware of the Club history, so many of my letters to him included stories and pictures. I always ended my letters with a thank you and a wish to be included on his list of potential buyers should he ever decide to sell. Dave was nice enough to respond to each yearly letter with a polite, "I don't think we have much interest (in selling) at this time."

> Pete & Nancy -   6-12-16
>
> Thanks for your letter -
> Hope the fishing was good
> this year -
> We've a good deal of
> interest in the property
> this past year from both
> the State & a local Gaylord
> couple. At one point we
> were considering it, but
> finally decided against it.
> We did put an easement
> on the property with the
> Headwaters Land Conservancy
> in Gaylord -
>
> Dave -

A typical yearly response from Dave Pottinger to my yearly letters thanking him for allowing us fishing access to the Club waters and expressing my continued interest in buying the Club property

As a family, we all ventured into the Club several more times before Mom passed away on April 1, 2015. In May, we held a family memorial on the Club property to celebrate Mom's life and the childhood she so loved growing up on the Pigeon. We placed a small cross beneath her birthday tree to honor a remarkable woman and the place she spoke of so often.

Mom's memorial at the Vanderbilt Club

Dear Mr. and Mrs. Pottinger,

I know my older brother Pete has corresponded with you over the years, and recently, in regards to our family using your Pigeon River property for our Mom's memorial service. I can't thank you enough for sharing it with us.

Though Mom's passing has been very difficult for all of us, having that sunny day on the banks of the Pigeon in the shadows of the old Club she loved so much, was an experience all of us needed and won't forget.

We brought picture albums of Mom's years at the Club and laughed and cried and remembered. We watched Dad tearfully rig up the old bamboo rod Mom had given him for his wedding gift and cast her favorite Royal Coachman into old familiar waters. We watched great grandchildren playing on the same paths Mom would have ridden her bike and chased her dogs and, slowly, this hurting, loving family begins to heal.

And now a small cross made of birch wood and pine boughs lays at the base of a long ago planted birthday tree. And a little girl has come home.

Thank you so much for your kindness and generosity.

Sincerely
David Mutch

Mom's birthday tree

Dad brought along the fly rod Mom gave him as a wedding present

We bought our Lovells property on the North Branch of the Au Sable River in October 2016, only after I thought the Club property would never be available to us. My initial name for the Lovells river cabin was "Plan B." However, Nan said no, thinking the neighbors might be offended; so, we named it "Coachman Lodge" in honor of Mom's favorite dry fly. The cabin was walk-in ready and the river was beautiful, peaceful, and fun to fish. Better yet, it was only a thirty-minute drive back to our favorite fishing spots in the Pigeon River Forest.

Royal Coachman Dry Fly – Mom's Favorite

I got home from work on February 13, 2019, and found Nan and Dad talking in the family living room in Lapeer. Nan greeted me with the usual conversation: "How was your day and who did you work on that I might know?" (I know, totally against HIPAA.) She also said that there was a phone message I should listen to and "you are not going to believe it!" Pottinger had called from Indiana and asked if I would call him back—so I did.

His conversation started out, "You probably know why I'm calling?" I really wasn't sure—I had only briefly corresponded with him during the past three years since Mom died. He went on to say that, over the years, he had had multiple offers to sell the property, either to local investors or the state of Michigan. I'm not really sure why he eventually called me. He didn't say and I didn't ask. But at this time, he and his wife had decided to sell the property and thought Nan and I might want to be back on the property as owners, if we were still interested. They thought our family connection to the Club property, a unique piece of land with a great local history, would serve it well.

We suddenly found ourselves with a very special and unexpected opportunity to not only continue with our many trips to the area, but also to continue with a family history that began there ninety years ago. While we are no longer "tives" (what Mom called the locals), we are by no means strangers. After some consideration, Nan and I decided to buy the Club property. My thoughts reflected back to the *Herald Times* article when Pottinger bought the Club property. If only I could see Mom's reaction now…

"The Club was just a part of another time. The members faded away and when the fire hit, I knew it was the end. I am so excited to see that someone else will be enjoying my old home now."

In Bill Ford's letter, he wrote, "How wonderful to hear that you have purchased the Vanderbilt Club property. It's a beautiful area, and I am sure the strong connection you share with the property through your grandparents and your mother makes it even more special to you. I wish you all the best as you bring your vision for this scenic property to fruition."

Months later, Nan and I had the pleasure to meet and walk the property with the Pottingers. He implied that his hesitancy to sell to the state, among other reasons, was his fear that all the big, beautiful red pines would be harvested, as is the state's practice for better elk management in the forest. He liked the thought that I might care for the property as he did—leaving it as natural as possible. He also said that I just kept "bugging" him. I like to interpret this as, "I showed extreme interest."

We hope that this land will continue in the family for many years to come. The Club property is much more than a location that shows up on a plat book. We truly bought a piece of our family history—a never-ending story—a story that has many chapters. Some chapters have already been written, but many more great chapters will follow. I've tried to tell you some facts so you could learn. I have told you a truth so you can believe. But most important, I have tried to tell you a story so it can live in your heart forever.

Mom and I hopefully have years to enjoy the property. I am going to seek a variance* with the DNR to rebuild Mom's old, tired cabin. It's perhaps ironic that the small, long ago abandoned cabin ("Mom's house") where she and Aunt Peggy slept, survived the devastating fire of 1971 that totally destroyed the large, beautiful log Vanderbilt Club house just next door. Perhaps her cabin was meant to survive until the family could return and now it gets a new life. Maybe brother Dave's letter to Pottinger says it best: "A little girl has come home." My thoughts ... I don't think she ever left. Nate, Kate, and Averie will add their own chapters as well as Andy, Beth, Natalie, and Elise.

Grandpa, Grandma, and Mom were literal "caretakers" of this small piece of the Pigeon. However, we are all small "caretakers" to the Lord's world—temporary stewards of his infinite works. So it is with humble gratefulness that this blessed opportunity allows our family to return as "caretakers" and "storytellers" to the land our mother loved so much. It's my hope that our family story continues forever.

Love to all, Pete and Nan

*A DNR Natural Rivers variance was necessary to rebuild Mom's cabin. The cabin was inside two hundred feet from the river and we were proposing to alter its grandfathered size. The variance was granted in July 2021 and construction began in spring 2022.

Dedications

My grandparents – Olga and Vern Dudd

Grandparents who set the stage.

Great parents who provided the experience, the example, and the great investment in their kids. It was always about family.

A dad who dedicated any spare time he had to getting us into the woods, on a lake or river, up to deer camp, behind a bird dog, on a ski hill, and exploring new places—mostly in a pop-up camper. He was the definition of hard work. The look and tears on Dad's face that day on the Pigeon when Nan and I shared the news of our new purchase was priceless. Dad suffered a stroke and passed away, October 7, 2020, shortly after his ninetieth birthday. He was able to briefly enjoy our new Club property and visited when he could but died shortly before I was finally granted a variance to rebuild Mom's cabin. Perhaps, had it not been for DNR approval delays brought on from all issues related to the COVID-19 shutdown, the entire process might have been completed much sooner and he could have fallen asleep on the porch to the sound of the river, just like he did almost seventy years ago.

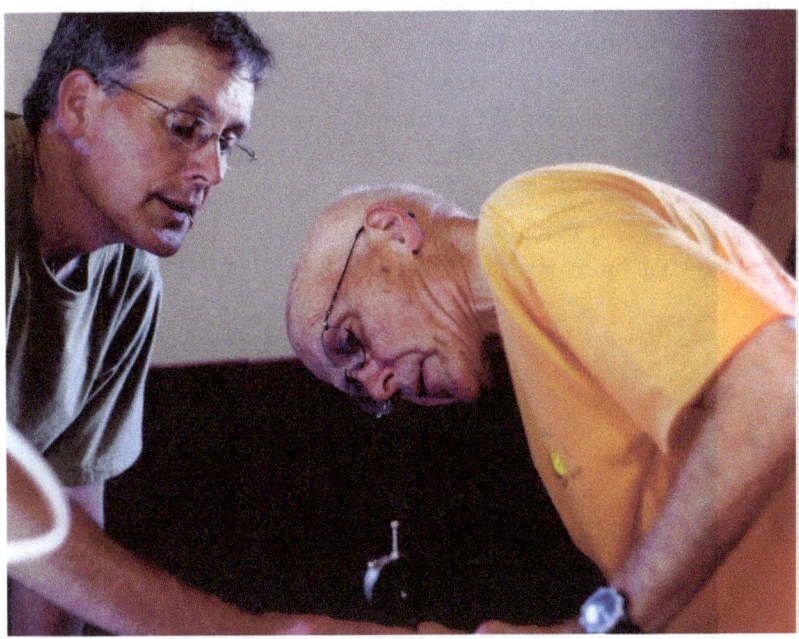

Dad and me at Jeff Wagner's bamboo fly rod class in Ohio

Mom and Dad

A mom who gave up her own career to be the best stay-at-home mom ever. Her days were filled with all things family—school, sports, church, and wishing us all her love as we moved out on our own. When it was time for college, my parents were always there to help me and my three siblings through a combined thirty-two years of college, resulting in four doctorate degrees. In addition, she helped Dad operate Robinsons Rexall Drug Store in Marlette, Michigan, for forty years. But no matter what Mom was doing, she always had time for stories about the Club and the Pigeon River.

Dad snowshoeing the Club property, February 2020

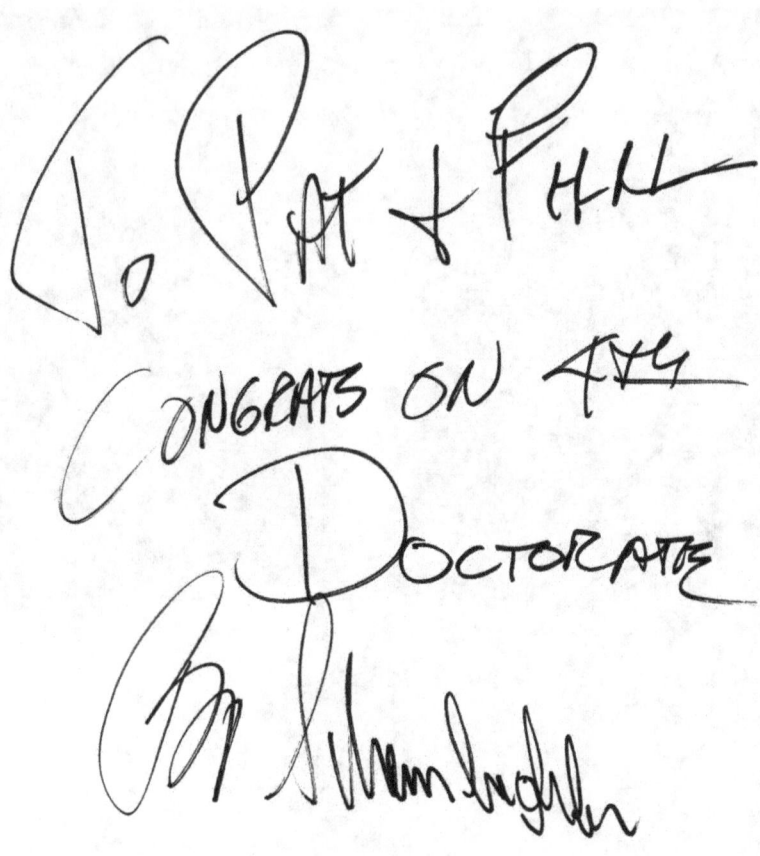

Bo Schembechler was the commencement speaker for brother Sam's graduation from the University of Michigan Dental School. Finally, Mom and Dad's last graduation ceremony they needed to attend.

A special gift and note from Mom to me

My brothers, sister, and I were extremely blessed. We grew up thinking everyone had a family like ours. The older we got, the more we realized how blessed and fortunate we were. It was a special day for Nan and me to read our surprise announcement to you on the banks of the Pigeon in June 2019.

One of our many annual fly fishing trips with Dad that took us all over the country. From Montana to Maine, to Arkansas and many places in between.
Slough Creek, Wyoming
From left to right: Sam, Dad, Dave, Becky, Me

I announced our Vanderbilt Club purchase to my siblings in June 2019 inside the footprint of the burned-out lodge. Dad was told the week before when we announced our purchase to the kids. Please note the wine bottle wrapped in aluminum foil on the small table. We had some great meals and bottles of wine on our trips. When mom joined us on our later trips, we asked her to wrap the wine bottles, keep score, and reveal the winner at the end of the week. Mom could be counted on to be a very impartial scorekeeper. Mom really didn't like wine, with the exception of her communion wine every other week at St. Paul Lutheran Church in Reed City. A wine bottle wrapped in aluminum foil still makes it to the table on many of our yearly fishing trips in memory of Mom.

Nan, who has been with me for most of my life. We were married forty-five years by the time we purchased the Club property. She has been the most dedicated and understanding wife, mom, grandmother, special education teacher, my best friend, and my great blessing. They say nobody is a perfect person, but she is about as close as you get. She figured out early on what most of her life's purpose and passion would be and what would bring her peace. All the rest was just "fluff." She often would say the scariest words out of my mouth were, "Nan, I've been thinking …" However, she didn't hesitate at all when the Club property came up for sale. It was all about family.

Nan at the Club picking blueberries

Nan with Dad on Sanibel Island, Florida

Pete Mutch | 143

"The Pigeon River Experience has been an incredible family journey." - Nan

My boys, Andy and Nate. We are so proud of you two. You are great sons, husbands, and dads now. You have learned how to appreciate what's really important in life and how our many blessings should not be taken for granted. Mom and I sit back and watch you and your families and feel extremely blessed.

Andy (right) and Nate (left), and me (taking picture), fishing trip. Yakutat, Alaska.

Andy, me, and Nate. Gangler's, Manitoba, Canada.

The daughters-in-law, Beth and Kate. You two have added so much joy to our lives. Thanks for being such great people, wives, moms, and the daughters we never had—blessed again.

Kate and Beth, camping

The grandkids, Natalie (10), Elise (8), and Averie (8). You are totally priceless. You fill our lives with so much joy: your school progress, sports, church, school plays, Mutch's Hidden Pines Christmas Tree Farm, surprise family trips, family time, Coachman Lodge, Indian Lake cabin, and now the Caretaker Club—blessed again, again, and again.

Natalie's first time fly fishing with me

Elise in waders with me

Averie and me exploring in our waders

Elise, Averie, and Natalie – this book was written for you!

The entire Caretaker Club family. Lovell's Bridge Walk 2018.

The future—most importantly. I pray for all those I haven't met yet and those I will never meet. May you become great caretakers as well!!!

Mutch love to you all,
Pete

Dad's memorial at the Vanderbilt Club. Mom and Dad are both buried in the Vanderbilt Evergreen Cemetery in front of Grandma and Grandpa Dudd and Grandma's brother, Lauist Anderson.

I wrote these words to the family. The words were hard to write and even harder to read out loud at Dad's cemetery service.

> *Yesterday, as I cried over Dad's casket, a million thoughts were racing through my mind. I mistakenly thought he would live forever. He always seemed to bounce back from any setback. He was not just my dad, he was my hero, mentor, and on my very short list of best friends. Not many sons can say this about their dad, so I consider myself very lucky. You could have a beautiful conversation with him even when his lips barely moved. The look in his eyes, his smile, or a nod of approval said it all. He was always around me even when he wasn't. He still is.*

So yesterday, as I sat by Dad's casket, I found myself being consoled by those around me. We all mourn his loss. As I sat there, my eyes kept staring at the beautiful picture Melissa had taken of Mom and Dad, hand in hand, walking away. The more I stared at it, another picture frame was beginning to appear alongside—no picture, just words. I'm quite sure no one else saw this. I suddenly found myself being consoled by someone else. As my tears began to clear, the tiny handwriting came into focus. This was an entry into Mom's daily journal that she always kept. It was dated 10-7-2020.

It said:

Phil-

The good Lord blessed me with you seventy years ago and I have personally thanked him many times. I loved every minute of our time together even though I haven't held your hand for five years. I really never left your side. I know how you surrounded yourself with my pictures. I know how much you missed me, and at times, how hard it was for you to keep going. You will discover that he has a grand, beautiful plan for all of us, even though our earthy wisdom can't totally explain it.

We were great together. We raised four beautiful kids who grew up to be our pride and joy. Our family was our top priority and we were always there for them, sharing their many joys and sorrows, celebrating in all their accomplishments, and accompanying them on many of their adventures. Our kids brought other blessings into our lives: daughters-in-law, a son-in-law, grandkids and great grandkids.

I don't know why you were chosen to stay behind. He didn't tell me. Maybe it was to get in a few more cherished fishing trips, have that last adventure with Art, to bale that last Christmas tree as grandpa to more kids than just your own, to finish the church's family tree project, to cut that last piece of wood for the fishing bench at Coachman Lodge, to return to Mom's birthday tree with a feeling of permanence, to wash that last dish with Becky, to take that last color tour with Dave and Lin, or to get those special calls from Sam. I really don't know the reason you stayed behind and he never said. When he told me to come get you, I was so excited for you to finally be with me. I have shared you with our very special family for five years, but he said it was finally time for you to be with me and all the special people that have left their earthly home and now rest with the Lord.

So put down your tool belt, turn off your scroll saw, put your truck keys on the shelf, hang up your fly rod, and follow me. I know you leave behind sad hearts and eyes full of tears. Our little family is very special so it makes it even harder to say goodbye. Time will heal. So Take My Hand and let me take you to that special home we all dream about. You can leave your earthly home and family with a smile on your face and a feeling of mission accomplished. Our earthly life is short but our heavenly life endures forever. All those who you leave behind will join us someday and share in our joy.

Your loving wife

Pat

Take My Hand
Mom and Dad at Longwood Gardens, Pennsylvania, 2008
Photo by Melissa Hopkins

Acknowledgements

I've talked about the Vanderbilt Club and my Pigeon River Country experience all my life. With the help of others, I finally decided to put it on paper.

I would like to thank Doug Weaver and his talented staff at Mission Point Press. I was excited to keep going after they read my initial manuscript – "this is going to be a dynamite book!"

I would like to thank Calla Scott for all her help with the many technical and computer demands as well as handling the communication between Mission Point Press and me.

A special thank you to my immediate and extended family. They gave me the time and space to write and helped fill in my occasional lapses in memory.

Finally, I am most grateful for my wife, Nancy, for her total support. For many reasons, as you, the reader, have discovered, without her, this book would never have been written. She also drew the sketches you see throughout the book.

Pete Mutch was born and raised in a small rural town in the "Thumb" of Michigan. He later went on to attend Alma College, Michigan State University, and the University of Michigan where he earned his B.S., M.S., and D.D.S. degrees respectively.

Along the way, he married his high school sweetheart, and homecoming queen, Nancy. He practices dentistry in Lapeer, Michigan – just down the road from their hometown. They raised two sons, have two great daughters-in-laws, and three precious granddaughters. Everyone loves to be outside in the woods, on a stream, in a canoe or camper. He and his family have always enjoyed the Pigeon River Forest and his very special family connection to the area. He enjoys fly fishing and more importantly, he loves the "environs" where trout are found. The old Vanderbilt Club put him right in the middle of it all.

www.ingramcontent.com/pod-product-compliance
Lightning Source LLC
Chambersburg PA
CBHW070320010526
44107CB00004B/375